WELCOME to my book about history . . . wait! Wait, where are you going? Come on back, because I'm going to let you in on a secret. Closer, closer . . . good.

Here goes: dates and battles and charters and treaties are *boring.* That's right, I said it! Boring! Fortunately, this isn't a book with dates and battles and charters and treaties, because that's not history.*

Nope. History is *stories.* True stories; better than fiction stories; crazy, incredible stuff-that-actually-happened stories!

Like, did you hear the one about the crazy Russian empress who used doves to set fire to an entire town? Or, how about the fact that court poisoner was an actual job in ancient Rome? Trust me, you're never gonna believe what the Trung sisters got their mom to do.

But you'll find out if you turn the page. So let's get to it. Let's go, hurry up! You're going to flip when you find out more about Ida B. Wells. (Hint: there's biting involved.)

Thanks for reading, and let's go!

—**Saundra**

---

* It's trivia. But don't tell your social studies teacher I said that. Don't worry, trivia comes in handy on game shows and college bowls.

50 UNBELIEVABLE WOMEN AND THEIR FASCINATING (AND TRUE!) STORIES

THEY DiD WHAT?

50 UNBELIEVABLE WOMEN

AND THEIR FASCINATING (AND TRUE!) STORIES

SAUNDRA MITCHELL

ILLUSTRATED BY CARA PETRUS

• Puffin Books •

PUFFIN BOOKS
An imprint of Penguin Random House LLC
375 Hudson Street
New York, New York 10014

First published in the United States of America by Puffin Books,
an imprint of Penguin Random House LLC, 2016

Text copyright © 2016 by Saundra Mitchell
Illustrations copyright © 2016 by Cara Petrus

LIBRARY OF CONGRESS CATALOGING-IN-PUBLICATION DATA
Names: Mitchell, Saundra.
Title: 50 unbelievable women and their fascinating (and true!) stories /
Saundra Mitchell.
Other titles: Fifty unbelievable women and their fascinating (and true!)
stories
Description: New York, New York : Puffin Books, 2016. | Series: They did
what? | Includes bibliographical references. | Audience: Grades 4–6. |
Audience: Ages 8–12.
Identifiers: LCCN 2015034065| ISBN 9780147518125 (paperback) |
ISBN 9780698410992 (e-book)
Subjects: LCSH: Women—Biography—Juvenile literature. | BISAC:
JUVENILE NONFICTION / Girls & Women.
Classification: LCC CT3203 .M615 2016 | DDC 920.72—dc23
LC record available at http://lccn.loc.gov/2015034065

ISBN 978-0-14-751812-5

Printed in the United States of America

1 3 5 7 9 10 8 6 4 2

Text set in Bell MT

This is for Mom, Aunt Mel, Aunt Jinni, Mom Bettis,
Ashley, Mom Sally, Donna, LaT, Mrs. Redman, Jane Yolen,
Tamora Pierce, and my HLM, Wendi.
Thank you for teaching me what
it is to be a woman, fearlessly. Love, Saundra.

To my family of strong women—especially Mom, G-Liz,
Aunt Nancy, Aunt Kate, Aunt Chris, Kristin, Hannah,
Olivia, and my sister, Jess. And to Dad and Steve, who have
loved being surrounded by us. —Cara

Contents

50 UNBELIEVABLE WOMEN AND THEIR FASCINATING (AND TRUE!) STORIES

Catherine the Great

Catherine the Great
1729–1796

With a nickname like "The Great," you know Catherine, Empress of All the Russias must have been pretty impressive.

In fact, she was so impressive that the people of Russia claimed her as their own. Kind of extraordinary, considering that that she wasn't even from there!

Born Sophie Friederike Auguste von Anhalt-Zerbst-Dornburg (say that three times fast!), Catherine was a minor princess in a small country called Prussia. She wasn't even the first or second in line for the throne at home. Instead, she was married off as a pawn to the emperor of Russia, Peter III.

Who, in fact, happened to be German. And really proud of it. Peter wasn't interested in ruling his new kingdom, and he made sure everybody knew it. He refused to learn to speak Russian, couldn't be bothered with the Russian people's needs, and definitely wasn't interested in learning their culture and heritage.

Stuck married to this snob, Catherine decided to try another way. Instead of blowing off her new country, she embraced it. In her heart, she stopped being Prussian and became Russian.

She changed her name to Ekaterina Alexeievna, which means Catherine, daughter of Alexei. She learned Russian, converted to their church, and got involved in the day-to-day concerns of the Russian people.

The Russians loved her for it. And she loved them. Peter, on the other hand, did exactly the opposite. He was supposed to be in charge, but he was more interested in playing practical jokes, hanging out with his German friends, and deciding disputes in Germany's favor. The Russian people were infuriated.

So Catherine did what she had to do. Fleeing the palace for the safety of the Ismailovsky Regiment, she asked them to protect her from Peter. They escorted her to their barracks, where bishops from the church waited to crown her sole empress of Russia.

Now crowned, and with the force of the military

behind her, she arrested her husband. He hadn't wanted to be a Russian emperor, so she made him sign a contract giving up all his rights to the throne.

Mysteriously, he died a few days later. People can't agree if it was suicide or murder, though many were willing to blame it on Empress Catherine!

Now the sole ruler of all the Russias, Catherine started her long, busy reign. She expanded their borders and opened relations with Western Europe and Japan. She built a national school system, including the first school for girls.

Somehow, she also found the time to write comedies and even her own memoirs. She reigned for thirty-four years, the longest rule of any female monarch in Russian history.

Catherine *chose* to be Russian. She embraced her new country, her new language, and her new people—and became the greatest (seriously!) empress in their history.

Joan Baez

Joan Baez
1941–

There was never any question about it: Joan Baez was going to make her voice heard in the world.

She grew up in an activist family, with two parents who passionately believed in fighting for social justice and civil rights. Dedicated to peace and nonviolence in a time of war, they converted to **Quakerism** when Baez was young.

Actively campaigning with her parents, Baez realized that her clear, resonating singing voice could spread the message that meant so much to her even farther.

As the United States slipped out of the Korean War and into the fight for African American civil rights at home, Baez and her guitar joined the peace movement.

Her passion for music with a message shone through. Arrested twice for speaking against sending young soldiers to fight in Vietnam, Baez said, "I went to jail for eleven days for disturbing the peace. I was trying to disturb the war."

Later, she held a free concert in Washington, D.C. Thirty thousand people turned out to hear her message of peace.

Baez continues to be a musical activist to this day. She's protested against the death penalty by singing "We Shall Overcome" at the gates of San Quentin Prison in California.

In 2004, she performed in the Slacker Uprising tour. Hosted by filmmaker Michael Moore, this tour traveled from college to college during the election season. Speakers and musicians urged young voters— the slackers in question—to rise up and vote.

Then in 2011, she performed in the Occupy Wall Street protest concert.

Though the folk music festivals of the 1960s are long gone, Baez still plays to protest. Her work as an advocate and activist rings out, as pure and rich as her music.

The message, to her, is simple: nonviolence is organized love.

FIRSTS!

In 1960, Sri Lanka (then Ceylon) elected the world's first female prime minister and head of state, Sirimavo Bandaranaike.

India elected the second, Indira Gandhi, and Israel the third with Golda Meir.

Argentina has the distinction of electing the first female president, Isabel Martínez de Perón. Her supporters called her La Presidente.

Madam C. J. Walker

Madam C. J. Walker
(Sarah Breedlove)
1867–1919

One day while washing clothes—that's what she did for a living at the time—Madam C. J. Walker had a realization. (Back then she was still named Sarah Breedlove, but we'll get to that in a minute!)

There wasn't much of a future in backbreaking manual labor. Sure, there were always clothes that needed to be washed—but was this really what she wanted to be doing for the rest of her life?

The answer was a resounding *no*!

A new possibility presented itself. Around the age of twenty, Walker discovered Annie Turnbo's Wonderful Hair Grower. Because her own hair was brittle and thinning, Walker started using the product. She liked it so much that she started selling it, door to door. It turned out she was a fantastic saleswoman.

After a while, she realized that she could make a lot more money if she invented her *own* hair tonics—so that's exactly what she did.

Changing her name from Sarah Breedlove to Madame C. J. Walker, she used herself as a before-and-after model for her company. Advertising in the burgeoning black press, she reached out directly to her customers with photographic proof that her products worked.

At the time, it was illegal for black Americans to start businesses that would compete with white businesses. That wouldn't be a problem, because what most interested Walker was working for—and with—other African American women. Those other companies weren't interested in making products for African American hair. Walker would fill that gap.

She tapped into French sophistication with her new name. Then she told people the recipe for her hair product came to her in a dream.* The ingredients she couldn't buy locally, she ordered from Africa.

At first, she sold to church groups and sewing circles. Word spread about her tonics, and their popularity grew.

*Historians believe it's more likely that she modified the Annie Turbo recipe for her own use.

To meet the demand, Walker opened a salon.

In fact, the demand was so great, she couldn't possibly do all the selling herself anymore. At the salon, she taught women how to use her product—then recruited them to sell it.

Before she knew it, Walker had salons in three cities, then more, then all across the United States! She built a state-of-the-art factory in Indianapolis, Indiana, and incorporated her company to protect it from outside speculators.

Working with universities and opening her own business college, Walker taught women how to create, own, and operate their own businesses.

Her washtub realization stayed at the forefront of her mind. She was determined to help other black women become financially independent business owners.

Money rolled in, and that made it possible for Walker to give generously to her community. She funded scholarships for black students and donated money to the black YMCA in Indianapolis.

It wasn't just donations, though. Walker went on lecture tours. She shared her business wisdom whenever she could. She was also an outspoken critic of racial discrimination.

When she wasn't building her empire, she was fueling the fight against **segregation** laws and **lynching** in the United States. Walker was never one to sit down and take it easy. There was always something more to be done.

Through hard work, canny business sense, and determination, Walker became the first female self-made millionaire in the country! What had started as a small home business in St. Louis now stretched not only across the country but also outside of the country. People in Haiti, Cuba, Colombia, and more couldn't get enough of Walker's hair tonics, either!

When she passed away in 1919, Walker left five thousand dollars to the NAACP—and her business empire to her daughter. Walker's factory in Indianapolis is now a theater.

The theater offers programs and lectures, plays and concerts. It's a place to congregate and a community that teaches the next generation to look up, and look forward.

It furthers the cause of social justice just like its namesake—and it still sells a small line of the hair-care products invented by the unforgettable Madam C. J. Walker.

HARD-CORE BATTLE QUEENS

In Vietnam, in the first century AD, Trung Truc and Trung Nhi lived under the rule of a cruel governor from the Chinese empire. Tired of seeing their people held hostage, abused, and worse, the Trung sisters wrote a fiery proclamation on a tiger's skin. Then they raised an army of eighty thousand to liberate the people of Vietnam.

From their army, the sisters trained thirty-six women to become generals (including their own mom!). They went to war, and in 40 AD, they liberated sixty-five fortresses and drove the Chinese invaders from their lands.

Ruth Bader Ginsburg

Ruth Bader Ginsburg

1933–

It's okay if you call Supreme Court Justice Ruth Bader Ginsburg the "Notorious RBG." She knows all about her fans' nickname for her, and she loves it.

Why shouldn't she? Ruth Bader Ginsburg attended law school, only one of fifty women in her entire class. Then when she graduated with honors, tied for first in her class, a judge refused to give her a job because she was a woman.

Ginsburg took a clerkship with another judge and cut a space for herself within the world of law. As an associate director on international procedure at Columbia Law School, Ginsburg learned Swedish and literally wrote the book on Swedish civil procedure.

Then she earned a position at Rutgers University as a law professor. At this point, she threw her energies into women's rights. Studying the history and the legal precedents, Ginsburg helped found the *Women's Law Review.* For the first time, women had a law journal that focused on their rights alone.

That wasn't enough, though. Ginsburg researched and, yep, again wrote the first casebook about gender discrimination against women.

Her very last case as a practicing lawyer argued that allowing women only to serve voluntarily on Missouri juries (instead of being legally required to, like men) was discriminatory.

As far as she was concerned, the message in that law was that the women of Missouri weren't important or necessary for a functional government.

President Jimmy Carter appointed Ginsburg to the U.S. Court of Appeals. Ginsburg served for thirteen years, until her nomination to the Supreme Court. Ginsburg was only the second woman and the first Jewish person to serve on the Supreme Court. How did she become the Notorious RBG?

Writing brilliant opinions and **dissents,** for one. Being outspoken about women's rights and the Supreme Court's approach to them, for another.

Fearlessly, she told the world that the court had

a blind spot when it came to women. But what really pushed her over the top? To a place where people make T-shirts and publish editorial cartoons about her, and run blogs and Tumblrs in her honor?

Her fierce determination to bring women to equality, no matter what, and a particularly fiery dissent in one particular case before the Supreme Court.

Ginsburg isn't afraid of speaking her mind, even when her opinion might not be a popular one. In one interview, the reporter asked how many women on the Supreme Court would be enough, and she didn't flinch.

"Nine," she said. "For most of the country's history, there were nine and they were all men. Nobody thought that was strange."

Corazon Aquino

Corazon Aquino
1933–2009

Everyone knew that María Corazon Cojuangco was special.

A bright girl from a political family in the Philippines, she was always at the top of her class. A valedictorian in elementary school, she left her native country to attend high school and college in the United States.

While she was there, she campaigned for Thomas Dewey in the 1948 presidential election. After earning degrees in mathematics and French, she returned to the Philippines for even more school—this time, law school. While she eventually planned to be a stay-at-home mom, she still valued her education.

Out of law school, she married Ninoy Aquino. He became the Philippines's youngest elected senator.

Aquino was proud of her husband but preferred to stay in the background. They had several young children by this point, so she didn't campaign with him. Her family was her job, and she was happy that way.

But in 1973, things changed in the Philippines. President Ferdinand Marcos decided he didn't want to follow the rules of their constitution anymore. He took over the country with his army and declared himself the permanent ruler.

Aquino's senator husband was sentenced to death for opposing Marcos. Rather than face the unjust sentence, Aquino, her husband, and their whole family fled to the United States. Later, she would say that the three years she spent there were among her happiest. Still, it was impossible for her to ignore what was happening back home in Manila.

Reluctantly, Aquino and her husband decided to return to the Philippines. Shortly after arriving, Aquino's husband was **assassinated**. For the first time in her life, Aquino stepped into the spotlight to give a passionate political speech. Becoming the leader of the People Power Revolution, Filipinos everywhere rallied around her.

Though she said she never wanted to be anything

but a housewife, Aquino ran for president and toppled Ferdinand Marcos's twenty-year dictatorship. She wrote a new, fair constitution and repaid her country's debts. She was determined to serve her people and to bring back social justice, human rights, and civil liberties.

She was such a good president that when her two terms were over, people encouraged her to run again. But that was against the new constitution, and worse, that's exactly what Marcos had done! Pointing out that she wasn't above the law, Aquino refused to run for a third term.

When the new president came into power, Corazon Aquino left not in a limousine, but driving her own family car. Happily, she went home to take care of her family, once again an ordinary citizen of her beloved country. The world, however, will always remember that she was extraordinary.

Vera Wang

Vera Wang

1949–

Most biographies don't start with growing up very wealthy in New York City, but Vera Wang's does.

Her father was a business owner, and her mother was a translator for the UN. Wang enjoyed elite private schools, fashion shows, dance lessons, and even an early career as a figure skater.

As a child and in her teens, Wang ice-skated competitively. A pairs skater, she competed at national and international contests. Twice, she and her partner placed fifth in the U.S. Nationals.

Gliding across the ice, Wang loved the way skating combined athletics and elegance. Yes, there was a lot of falling down, but Wang learned an important life lesson. To learn to skate, she *had* to fall down. But if she wanted to *keep* skating, she had to get up and try again.

Wang saw the 1968 Olympics as her goal. Skating harder than ever, she desperately wanted to represent the United States in Grenoble, France.

Unfortunately, Wang and her partner faced stiff competition and failed to secure a place on the team. (Peggy Fleming, who *did* make the team, went on to win the United States' only gold medal in the Games that winter.)

That was a long fall down, in a really big way. The question Wang had to ask herself was, What would she do when she got up again?

College to start with. She studied in the United States and France, ultimately earning a degree in art history at Sarah Lawrence. From there, Wang considered going to design school.

Nope, family told her. Get a job instead!

So that's what she did—securing an interview at *Vogue*. Landing an editorial position, she worked her way up to senior editor. For seventeen years, she oversaw spreads for one of the world's most influential fashion magazines.

When the editor in chief position opened, Wang wanted it. She applied and was disappointed when the job went to someone else. Another long fall down—Wang left *Vogue* to work at Ralph Lauren as a design director.

It wasn't until she went looking for her own bridal gown that Wang finally found her calling. Disinterested in poufy princess gowns, Wang found it frustrating that there were no sleek dresses that suited her taste.

She could have settled. Instead, she designed her own dress.

A year later, she opened her first bridal studio in New York. People loved her designs. Soon, she was designing dresses for Hollywood red carpets and superstar weddings. Oh yeah—she also designed figure-skating costumes.

That's right. Wang never gave up skating *completely*. She still enjoyed going out on the ice. And she shot to fame as a designer when skater Nancy Kerrigan wore one of her costumes at the 1994 Olympics. (How about that, Wang got into the Olympics after all!)

Now she runs a billion-dollar fashion empire that offers everything from perfume to casual wear, from designer glasses frames to, of course, custom-made wedding gowns. Learning to get up after a fall helped Wang achieve her success.

And like a figure skater, she still swirls around and around—looping her past with her present to make a beautiful future.

Minnie Spotted Wolf

Minnie Spotted Wolf

1923–1988

Never one to take it easy, Minnie Spotted Wolf spent the first part of her life working on her family's ranch in Montana.

A member of the Blackfoot Tribe, Spotted Wolf delivered equipment and supplies for the ranch in a two-ton truck. She spent a lot of time cutting and setting fence posts. When the ranch got new horses, she trained and tamed them. Barely five feet tall, Spotted Wolf was plenty big enough to accomplish all that and more.

At the start of World War II, she felt a calling. Something told her that it was her duty to serve the United States during wartime, and that she should join the Marines to do it. The first recruiter she talked to discouraged her. He told her war was no place for a woman.

Disappointed, Spotted Wolf returned home. Though she still longed to join the military, she resigned herself to a life at home, doing the same jobs she'd always done.

In 1943, the Marines established the Women's Reserve. Spotted Wolf was elated. There was finally a place for her! Just as she planned to join, her father died in an accident.

Torn, Spotted Wolf almost decided to stay at the ranch for good. However, her family knew how much this dream meant to her, and they encouraged her to sign up.

She did! And she became the first Native American woman ever to enlist in the Marine Corps.

This Blackfoot woman found herself growing even stronger in boot camp. After a lifetime on the ranch, she considered this training hard, but not *too* hard.

After that, she learned to drive and operate even more heavy equipment. Then she learned how to fix it!

Throughout the rest of the war, Spotted Wolf transported weapons and troops and operated heavy equipment for the war effort. The Marines wrote a comic book about her accomplishments, and Spotted Wolf served her four-year tour with pride.

Afterward, she went home to Montana—but not to work the ranch. Instead, she surprised everyone with her next calling—teaching! This veteran headed off to college and earned her degree in elementary education.

Four years as a Marine, Spotted Wolf then spent *twenty-nine years* in her second career as a school teacher. She loved her students, and she loved learning. She continued to take college courses at night, even as she taught during the day. She wanted to earn her doctorate.

After working on a ranch and serving in the military, Minnie Spotted Wolf was tough enough to take on education. And you know what? The kids in her classes knew they had to behave. After all, their teacher wore combat boots!

Tegla Loroupe

Tegla Loroupe

1973–

Her father didn't want her to run. He said it was unladylike.

Good thing that Tegla Loroupe ignored him. If she hadn't, she wouldn't have become the first African woman to win the New York City Marathon. And she wouldn't have become an ambassador for the United Nations. Or contributed to thousands of warriors abandoning their weapons and embracing peace.

Born in Kutomwony, Kenya, Loroupe had twenty-four siblings! She was expected to spend much of her time helping to care for her family. Not initially an athlete, Loroupe started running to get places. Specifically, she had a ten-kilometer run to get to school every day. (That's a little more than six miles!)

It was at school that people realized Loroupe had

a gift for racing. Regularly, she won eight-hundred- and fifteen-hundred-meter races against runners much older than herself. Loroupe had only the support of her mother. Even the Kenyan Athletics Federation thought she was too little and delicate to compete.

So, Loroupe entered a cross-country race in 1988, and won—barefooted! At that point, the athletics federation had to take notice. Loroupe competed nationally and internationally. The next year, she won her first pair of running shoes. She saved them for special occasions— perfectly happy to run in her bare feet.

Soon, Loroupe was winning races and setting records. She won the Goodwill Games in 1994 and 1998; in the IAFF World Championships, she took home bronze medals.

Her fame grew when she won the New York City Marathon in 1994 and 1995. She was the first African woman to do it, and at this point, she couldn't be stopped.

Loroupe swept the Rotterdam Marathon, the Berlin Marathon, the Zevenheuvelenloop 15K in the Netherlands, the Lisbon Half Marathon, the Paris Half Marathon, and the Osaka International Ladies Marathon. And more!

She competed in the Sydney Olympics in 2000, in spite of suffering a bad case of food poisoning. Even though she didn't perform well, she thought it was important to try anyway.

In 2006, the United Nations named her an Ambassador of Sport. Back home in Kenya, she created the Tegla Loroupe Peace Foundation. Building schools and opening athletics up to the next generation is its primary focus.

Plus, every year, she sponsors a peace race in Kenya. Bringing together high-powered athletes and powerful warriors of rival tribes, this race always has an extra message. Supporting peace efforts, encouraging community, and sponsoring rural schools—in 2011, the motto of the Peace Race was "No to guns, yes to pens!"

So it's a good thing that Tegla Loroupe didn't listen to her father. She had a lot of work to accomplish and couldn't be dissuaded. To stop her, you'd have to catch her—and she's a world-record holder, three times over!

Marie Curie

Marie Curie
1867–1934

A brilliant scientific mind, Marie Curie earned three degrees in a time when her native Poland wouldn't even let her attend its universities.

Forced to leave home to follow her passion for science, Curie found herself in Paris, at the Sorbonne. There, Curie earned **licentiateships** (a kind of degree greater than a bachelor's degree, but lesser than a master's) in mathematical sciences and physics.

Later, at the University of Paris, she earned her doctor of science, and became the first female professor of general physics there.

You probably know all about Marie Curie's experiments with radium. After all, it won her not one, but two, Nobel Prizes—in two different fields! Stories about how Curie carried radioactive isotopes in her pockets are popular, and she engineered the first radiation treatments for cancer patients.

What you probably don't know is that Curie was so dedicated to using her scientific discoveries for good that she went to war to put her new technology to use.

Studying anatomy, radiology, and automotive mechanics, she built a petite Curie: a portable X-ray bus! She drove it to battlefield hospitals during WWI, providing much needed medical care to injured soldiers.

One petite Curie was hardly enough. The Red Cross appointed her director of their radiology service. In turn, Curie built a radiology center, engineered the use of radon to sterilize wounds, and oversaw the production of twenty more portable X-ray buses.

Then she personally trained women as X-ray aides—after all, she knew they could more than handle it!

Poland refused to let her study, and Paris refused to acknowledge her brilliant discoveries. Too bad for them. They missed their chance to be associated with a genius who discovered radium and polonium, and pioneered nuclear medicine.

They Did What?

To Marie Curie, knowledge, not acknowledgment, was the most important thing. She didn't patent any of her discoveries: she felt they belonged to science.

MAD, BAD, AND DANGEROUS TO KNOW

Through the years, people have had different opinions on alcohol. Benjamin Franklin said that beer was proof that the Almighty loves us and wants us to be happy. On the other hand, Carrie Nation thought the Almighty personally charged her with the task of ridding the world of demon alcohol.

Oh yeah, her personal calling from heaven encouraged her to do that ridding with a hatchet. Of course!

Nation marched into bars and saloons to carry out her "hatchetations." She would inform the patrons, "Men, I have come to save you from a drunkard's fate!" Then she'd save them by chopping up the bar, its fixtures, and most important, all the barrels containing liquor. Sometimes, she'd sing hymns or pray while she worked.

Arrested and jailed several times, Nation didn't let the law deter her. In fact, she created a newspaper and a newsletter to spread her message of temperance. She had plenty of followers, which was good. Her hatchetations led to her arrest more than thirty times. Proceeds from souvenir hatchet sales and speaking fees paid her legal bills.

Celia Cruz

Celia Cruz
1925–2003

With gorgeous gowns, wild wigs, and stunning stage shows, Celia Cruz was considered the Queen of Salsa.

Born in Havana, Cuba, Cruz started her singing career in her teens—and her father wasn't happy about it. He wanted her to go to school and become a teacher. But Cruz's aunt realized she had a rich, unique singing voice, and encouraged her to go into music.

Unsure, Cruz continued with her schooling until one of her teachers pointed out that she'd be much more successful at singing than teaching. That cinched it!

In the early years of her career, Cruz entered singing contests—and won! They were sweet victories; not only did they encourage her to keep following her dream, the prizes were usually cakes and other confections.

From there, she moved on to clubs and cabarets in Havana, the glittering capital city. It was an amazing time to be a Cuban, and Cruz shot to fame on the radio.

Then in 1959, Fidel Castro took control of the government. The new Communist **regime** changed everything. This was no longer a Cuba that Cruz recognized.

She left to give a concert in Mexico and never went home again. From there, she moved to New York, but she refused to give up her Cuban identity. She brought her beloved salsa music with her and soon found fame in the United States as well.

Her passion for music and Cuba combined into her catchphrase, ¡Azúcar!—Sugar! It started out as a joke she told during her concerts. To give her horn section a break, she'd share a story about the way she took her coffee—the way *all* Cubans took their coffee, according to her.

Eventually, she didn't have to tell the story anymore. She would greet her fans with ¡Azúcar! and her fans would shout it back.

Her saucy horns and snappy salsa beat inspired the next generation of musicians. Jennifer Lopez, Gloria Estefan, and Pitbull consider Cruz one of their musical mentors and role models.

Though Celia Cruz never returned to Cuba, she never left it, either. In her music, she always brought the flavor of her home country with the rhythm and beat and swag. And of course, always a little sugar to make it sweet.

¡Azúcar!

Tina Fey

Tina Fey

1970–

It would be easy to say that award-winning actress, comedian, and writer Tina Fey is just funny. After all, she shot to fame on one of the most famous comedy shows in history, *Saturday Night Live.*

Hired out of college as one of the *SNL* staff writers, she became the first female head writer in the show's history by 1997. Little by little, she appeared in front of the camera as well.

Co-anchoring one of the most popular segments on the program, *Weekend Update*, Fey delivered searing, hilarious commentary on world news. It seemed to surprise some people to hear such biting, clever comedy coming from such a sunny person.

It shouldn't have. Fey has always had a bigger message. When her college held auditions for a military play that featured no female roles, she was furious. She and a friend raided the prop closet for rifles, boots, and helmets.

Then they marched onto stage during the all-male auditions. Performing a routine about female soldiers of World War II, they made their point, then marched off.

Early in her career at *Saturday Night Live*, Fey was disappointed when the male producers of the show decided to let a man play a female character instead of one of the talented women in the cast.

As Fey rose through the ranks, she changed the face of the program. By the time she left, no one would have put anyone but a woman in a woman's part on the show.

Writing for her own sitcom, Fey had the opportunity to put women first, and she did. *30 Rock* was a hit—Fey won Emmy after Emmy for her portrayal of Liz Lemon on the show.

At the same time, she wrote and produced the film *Mean Girls*, based on the book *Queen Bees and Wannabes* by Rosalind Wiseman. The film catapulted Rachel McAdams and Lindsay Lohan to fame, and became a piece of pop culture history.

If you're still trying to make fetch happen, and wear pink on Wednesdays, it's because Tina Fey knew exactly how to write about young women in a way that was honest, smart, and real. And also? Very, very funny.

Just not *only* funny.

Emperor Wu Zétian

Emperor Wu Zétian
624–705

There's a saying that history is written by the victors. Sometimes that means history is *rewritten* for political reasons.

Depending on whom you ask, the only female emperor of China was either (a) an incredibly vicious opportunist who murdered anyone who got in the way of her rise to power. Or (b) a progressive, forward-thinking emperor who opened her government to all people, commissioned a history of notable women, and improved the economy.

Chances are, Wu Zétian was both. Starting out as one of the emperor's **concubines**, she proved herself to be an able partner and administrator. Her gift for **diplomacy** came in handy. When the emperor died, all of his concubines shaved their heads and entered a convent. They weren't ever supposed to leave.

Wu, however, had other ideas. She struck up a friendship with the *new* emperor. Within weeks, she charmed him enough to become one of his concubines. Her influence grew; he elevated her to his equal and took her advice on all things. Then he conveniently died and left a power vacuum.

That vacuum needed to be filled, and Wu was up to the task. Sure, to make a path to the throne, she *allegedly* set up two of her own sons (one, she executed; the other, she framed for treason). It's entirely *possible* she strangled her own infant daughter and pinned the crime on the only other concubine in the palace with any power.

It's a *fact*, however, that she started taking comments and ideas from anyone willing to offer them. She even created anonymous comment boxes in the palace, to encourage people's input. Reforming the political system, Wu instituted a civil service exam and job interviews. That way the best person for the job, no matter whether noble or a humble farmer, would get the job.

She expanded the Tang dynasty and secured its rule, mostly in peacetime. China grew during her reign. It became the largest empire in the history of the world. On her command, a history of powerful women was written, and mothers were celebrated equally with fathers.

The way history looks at Emperor Wu is skewed, however. She upset the social order in China. As a woman, she was expected to serve, not to be served. No matter how popular and prosperous her rule, the establishment couldn't encourage that kind of behavior. They played up Wu's worst traits and downplayed her greatest successes.

History, when it's written, is written by the victors. That is never more evident than on her tombstone. Erected during her lifetime, Wu left the face of the stone uncarved. She did this, as all the emperors had done before her. It was customary to leave it blank. It was the next emperor's job to fill it in—the new emperor paying respects to the last.

That's not what happened when Emperor Wu died at the age of eighty-three. Though history was unable to erase the memory of Wu Zétian, to this day, her tombstone remains blank.

Elizabeth "Bessie" Coleman

Elizabeth "Bessie" Coleman

1892–1926

Pretty much everyone knows who Amelia Earhart is. The other name in early aviation you should know is Elizabeth "Bessie" Coleman.

When young pilots and soldiers came back from World War I, Coleman was fascinated by their air-battle stories. There were feats of courage and bravery, terrifying **dogfights** that made them fear for their lives. Flying meant freedom, even if it *was* dangerous. (In fact, maybe *because* it was dangerous!)

The problem was, Coleman was both black and a woman. In 1918, most flying schools refused to accept women—let alone African American women. Still, Coleman couldn't stop dreaming of soaring through the clouds. She would not be stopped!

So she took all of her savings and went to France.

The schools there were happy to teach her to fly. Seven months of training flew by, most of it in biplanes with failing engines. One of her classmates actually died during training. Though frightened, Coleman refused to turn back. She earned her pilot's license in June of 1921.

When she came back to the United States, people celebrated her achievement. The standing ovation she got at a musical performance was nice—but flying was the best thing in the world. Coleman joined air shows, flying stunts and maneuvers to shock and delight the crowds below.

Since she had proved it was possible, Coleman encouraged other African Americans to get their pilot's license, too. She didn't want anyone else to have to go a world away to learn the joys of aviation, like she had. And she very pointedly refused to perform shows unless African Americans were permitted to be part of the audience.

For five years, Coleman lived her dream as a stunt pilot. Famous from coast to coast, she stunned and delighted audiences everywhere.

In 1926, she bought a two-seater plane. She wanted to do a stunt where she leaped from the plane and floated to the earth on a parachute. Her manager and mechanic would stay behind to land the plane safely. The problem was, it was a used plane. It wasn't in very good condition. Though Coleman's family and friends begged her to stick with her tried-and-true, she refused.

She was a stunt pilot, and people wanted new, amazing thrills. So when she arrived in Jacksonville, Florida, for the next show, she had to practice. Ascending with her mechanic in the second seat, Coleman was flying high. Looking over the side of the plane, she studied the airfield. She had to figure out the best place to jump.

Suddenly, a wrench got stuck in the controls. The plane spiraled wildly, then plunged toward the earth. Without a seat belt, Coleman toppled from the plane and fell to her death.

The first African American lady of aviation left tens of thousands of mourners behind. Not only that, she inspired many young pilots to follow her. There has been a stamp featuring her face, there's a Bessie Coleman Club of black female pilots, and every year, black pilots from Chicago fly over her grave in tribute.

Though she lived a short life, Coleman lived a thrilling one—up among the clouds, flying and free.

Christine de Pisan

Christine de Pisan

1364–1430

The rules for women were different in the fourteenth and fifteenth centuries. Denied an education, most women spoke their own language, but few could read it. Even fewer could write.

Christine de Pisan was a notable exception. Born in Florence, she wrote and spoke Italian, of course. And moving with her family to the French court of Charles V, she learned to speak and write Middle French as well.

There, she was allowed to study math, science, and history. On top of that, she learned Greek and Latin, and read her fill of classical literature. If she'd been a shepherdess, she wouldn't have been this fortunate. Born into a noble family, though, she had many advantages that other women didn't—and she appreciated that!

Another thing that set Christine de Pisan apart was that she supported herself as a writer in a time when women simply didn't become writers.

Widowed after ten years of marriage, the twenty-five-year-old de Pisan (yep, she got married at fifteen!) suddenly had to support her three children on her own. Because she'd spent so much time in the French royal court, de Pisan knew how popular poems and ballads were.

She picked up her pen and wrote her very first ballad, a dark and romantic remembrance of her late husband. People loved it, so she wrote more. Over the years, she penned strictly constructed sonnets and **rondeaux**, easygoing and lively poems, and plenty of love ballads.

Because women generally weren't allowed to have an education, de Pisan was a novelty: a woman who could write. More important, she was a woman who wrote *well*. And prolifically: in poetry alone, she wrote more than three hundred pieces!

However, de Pisan didn't hold herself apart from the literary world. When another author wrote a **scathing** book that **satirized** the way he thought women behaved, de Pisan replied.

In her opinion, he had no idea what women were really like, because women weren't generally allowed to speak up. She took apart his depictions with relish.

Soon, others got into the debate, and the incident became known as the Querelle du Roman de la Rose. In English, that means the fight over the Rose book.

Inspired by this debate, de Pisan wrote the first of two books about women's real lives, thoughts, and feelings. *The Book of the City of Ladies* was the first, followed by *The Book of Three Virtues*. Both huge successes, these books offered a stark contrast to the standard literature of the day.

Late in life, de Pisan retired to a convent when war threatened the king's royal court. That had been her home for all her life, and it frightened her to see it vulnerable. She stopped writing entirely, except for one last, blazing poem.

Christine de Pisan was inspired to write once more about an extraordinary woman making history. The only author who wrote about this subject during her lifetime, de Pisan is also the only author to write about her in her own language. She alone captured the thrilling liberation of Orleans by a country maiden, as it happened.

That's right, de Pisan finished her career with one last ballad about Joan of Arc.

Annie Jump Cannon

Annie Jump Cannon

1863–1941

Her mother introduced her to the stars, and Annie Jump Cannon fell in love.

She learned the constellations as a child, then followed the stars to Wellesley College in 1884. Studying astronomy and physics, Cannon found herself learning from Sarah Whiting, a famed professor of her day.

After graduation, Cannon had no expectations of taking a job in astronomy. Those belonged to men, and it would be a rare and special circumstance for a woman to be considered at all. So she spent the next decade of her life traveling and devoting herself to music.

After traveling to Europe to photograph a solar eclipse, Cannon fell ill with scarlet fever. Today, we know that scarlet fever is an allergic reaction to a strep throat infection. It's easily cured with antibiotics. Unfortunately, in the 1890s, things were very different. Penicillin wouldn't be discovered for another forty years.

Cannon was lucky to survive her bout of scarlet fever, but she emerged from it almost completely deaf. Sadly, two years later, her mother died. Changed by illness and mourning the loss of the woman who had given her the stars, Cannon retreated to them.

She went to Radcliffe College to take graduate courses in astronomy. Because of her hearing impairment, she was considered a special student. That was fine by Cannon. It meant she got to study and work with the stars she loved so much.

From there, an astronomer from Harvard hired her to be part of his "computing" team. They weren't working with the Internet or WiFi—they were trying to catalog every single star in the sky. Every single one!

Cannon had a gift for star classification. Building on the work of sister astronomers Nettie Farrar and Williamina Fleming, Cannon refined the star classification scale, based on the temperature of the star. Astronomers still use this scale today; it's known as the Harvard spectral classification scheme now.

Though female astronomers at Harvard were paid less than the secretaries, Cannon was happy to be immersed in her work. Over the course of her career, she classified more than three hundred thousand stars, and discovered more than three hundred.

Time named her the "Census Taker of the Sky." The first female officer of the American Astronomical Society, Cannon's other firsts included the first honorary degree offered by Oxford University to a woman and the first woman to win the Draper Gold Medal, an award granted by the United States National Academy of Sciences in the category of astrophysics.

Because she had been discouraged early on from finding a career in astronomy, Cannon founded the Annie J. Cannon Award, to acknowledge and encourage distinguished female astronomers. This award is granted every year—to this day!

When you look at the sky, think of Annie Jump Cannon. At least three hundred of those stars have names because of her. And the rest—well, she'd love you to fall in love with them, too!

Lea Salonga

Lea Salonga
1971–

When Lea Salonga sings, people listen. They always have.

When she was a little girl growing up in the Philippines, Salonga got her start early in the capital city of Manila. Only seven years old, she starred in Repertory Philippines's production of *The King and I*. Once audiences met this powerhouse talent, they wanted more.

Salonga dove into musical theater full time. Scoring role after role, she appeared in some of the world's favorite Broadway musicals. Her voice led her to roles in *Annie, Fiddler on the Roof,* and *The Fantastiks*.

When she was ten, she recorded her first album. Going on to star in a string of family movies, Salonga earned nominations as best child actress from the

Aliw Awards and the Filipino Academy of Movie Arts and Sciences Awards.

Hosting her own music show, *Love, Lea*, Salonga was already wildly popular at home when she went to New York to audition for Broadway. Competing against a friend from Repertory Philippines for the role of Kim in *Miss Saigon*, Salonga was only seventeen when she earned the starring role.

For most people, Salonga *was* Kim. There was no *Miss Saigon* without her! She created the role and owned it in a way no other actor ever would. Critically acclaimed for her performance, Salonga won award after award—the Tony, awarded for best theater performances in the United States; the Olivier, the same, but for UK productions; and more!

Even when she moved on to other musicals, producers invited her back to *Miss Saigon* as a special treat for audiences. Twelve years after she originated the role, she returned to Broadway to close the show after its incredible twelve-year run.

After *Miss Saigon*, Salonga became the first Filipino woman to play Éponine in *Les Misérables*. She recorded albums, went on tour, and found time to make a few movies as well.

Even if you haven't seen her in them, you might have heard her. She reflected on a whole new world in two different Disney films.

Indeed! Salonga provided the singing voice for Mulan and *Aladdin*'s Princess Jasmine! She said it was always a dream to become a Disney princess.

After playing Princess Jasmine, she said the role made her entire year. Then when she was invited to audition to play Mulan, it made her life!

With a voice that carried her all the way to Broadway and back, Lea Salonga continues to be a star on stage and screen. But she's never forgotten her start.

She makes her home in Manila, where she presides as one of the judge mentors on *The Voice Philippines*.

Perhaps she hopes to find the next Lea Salonga among the contestants!

Susan La Flesche Picotte

Susan La Flesche Picotte

1865–1915

Part of the Omaha Nation of Nebraska, Susan La Flesche Picotte was born in a tepee, sent away to boarding school, and eventually became the first Native American physician in the United States.

Born at a time when white settlers were pushing Native tribes from their ancestral lands, Picotte deftly managed to be a part of both worlds. Her parents played a role in that.

Though they raised their children among the Omaha, they sent them to an English-speaking boarding school. It was their hope that they would learn how to associate with the new settlers.

When Picotte returned home, she realized that she wanted to help her people. Things were changing so fast for the Plains Indians. **Industrialization** and

relocation brought many new diseases and illnesses to the Omaha Nation.

When she was sent to sit with a sick Omaha woman, Picotte found her calling. She didn't have any medical training at the time. There was nothing she could do but send for the local physician. He promised to come—but never did. Probably, Picotte thought, because the woman was an Indian— not important to a white doctor.

Never again, Picotte decided. Few colleges accepted female students at the time, and even fewer accepted students of color. This didn't stop Picotte, though.

With the help of friends, and tuition assistance from the Connecticut Indian Foundation, Picotte enrolled in the Women's Medical College of Pennsylvania.

Graduating at the top of her class, Picotte could have gone anywhere as a doctor. Everywhere, there were hospitals and clinics clamoring for trained physicians. Picotte chose to go back to the Omaha Reservation.

At first, the Omaha were suspicious. She was a woman, after all. Could a woman really be a doctor?

Curing a sick little boy, Picotte proved she could. As she opened her practice, she often saw more than a hundred patients a day. She turned away no one—Indian or white.

It wasn't an easy calling. When male doctors were making five thousand dollars a year, she made only five hundred. Sometimes she worked twenty hours a day or more, and made dozens of house calls in all kinds of weather.

Picotte dreamed of building a hospital, and who could blame her? She practiced medicine in a one-room building that was only twelve feet wide and sixteen feet long!

That dream came true in 1913. Unfortunately, by then, Picotte wasn't well enough to practice at the hospital. But she could see the difference it made in the reservation's health.

Though Picotte never had a chance to settle into a cushy, comfortable life, she did exactly what she set out to do. From the time she was a girl, all she wanted was to make a difference.

Today, the Dr. Susan La Flesche Picotte Memorial Hospital in Walthill, Nebraska, still cares for the people of the Omaha Reservation. Picotte made a difference a hundred years ago; her legacy continues to make one today.

Halet Çambel

Halet Çambel
1916–2014

Born in Turkey in 1916, Halet Çambel was more likely to grow up to become a wife and mother than she was to become an Olympic athlete and archaeologist. But Çambel wasn't super interested in what she was *supposed* to do.

A talented fencer, she competed in the 1936 Olympics. In more than one way, she stood apart from her competitors. Not only was she a woman, she was the first Muslim woman to take part in the games. She also refused to meet privately with German führer Adolf Hitler.

Like many women of her time, Çambel had to leave home to get her degree. Off to France she went, to the Sorbonne, a university in Paris. There, she completed her degree in archaeology—then took her knowledge back to her home country of Turkey. The University of Istanbul couldn't help but admire Çambel. They admitted her there, where she earned her doctorate.

Çambel was fascinated with her country's distant past. This led her to help translate ancient Hittite hieroglyphics, allowing the modern world finally to read some of the oldest writings in the world.

As part of the early cradle of civilization, Turkey had archaeological sites that dated back more than four thousand years. Many people were careless with these irreplaceable sites. The government wanted to pry statutes and **steles** from the walls of ancient cities and put them in their museums.

That wouldn't do. "How can you move a house?" Çambel asked. "How can you move a two-ton statue?"

She fought hard to preserve the archaeological sites as they were. How else would people have the chance to understand their ancient heritage in the city of Karatepe if it wasn't there to visit? She convinced the government instead to build a museum *at* Karatepe, an open-air exhibit for all Turkish people to enjoy.

Every time someone threatened the preservation of Turkey's historical wonders, Çambel stepped in.

From convincing goat herders to switch out their flocks for sheep (the goats were stripping the pine forests and leaving the land vulnerable to erosion) to helping village weavers recover the ancient art of natural dyes for their fibers, Çambel did everything she could to preserve and celebrate the long history of her home country.

Her next battle against the government was a soggy one. The government had decided to dam the Ceyhan River. This would have flooded hundreds of priceless archaeological sites. Though she couldn't stop the dam entirely, Çambel did convince the government to create a smaller reservoir to save those sites.

All her life, Halet Çambel ignored what people thought she should do and fought for what she thought was right. Now, she's remembered as an Olympian, an archaeologist, and a scientific hero—a Turkish national treasure.

Ida B. Wells

Ida B. Wells

1862–1931

Sometimes, things change only when you force people to listen. Ida B. Wells refused to lower her voice in a time when everyone wanted her to whisper.

Born to enslaved parents, Wells and her family were **emancipated** in 1865. Wells's parents told her that her job was to get an education. It was finally legal for African Americans to learn to read and write. As far as her parents were concerned, it was *required*.

Wells grew up listening to her father advocate for racial equality. The war had changed much, but it hadn't changed people's attitudes, fears, and prejudices. At the age of sixteen, Wells went east to go to college.

Then a terrible epidemic killed both of her parents, leaving Wells and her five siblings orphaned. Abandoning her university career, Wells returned home to be the woman of the house. To support her family, she dressed herself to look as old as possible and landed a teaching job.

During the week, she would ride six miles to teach at her school, then come home on the weekends to cook, clean, and iron. It wasn't an easy life. Continuing her education during summers, Wells went on to qualify to teach at the city schools.

That might have been where she stayed, if not for an incident in 1884. Among the things that hadn't changed since the Civil War, **segregated** businesses and facilities were distressingly common. Whites could work, play, or shop anywhere. African Americans had to use "black-only" amenities.

That included where people could sit on the train. On a trip, with her first-class ticket, Wells took a seat in the nonsmoking ladies' car. A few moments later, the conductor appeared. He demanded that Wells move to the smoking car. It was second-class and reserved for African Americans.

Wells refused to move. When the conductor tried to force her out of the first-class car she'd paid for, she fought back. She braced her feet against the seats and held on tight. Then she bit the conductor on the hand—

hard! It took four men to remove her from the train.

Afterward, she sued the train company for damages—and won! It was the first time an African American had won a civil case against an American company. Wells wrote about the experience for a local church newspaper. The story was so well received, the newspaper asked her to keep writing for them.

She did, and soon papers around the country ran her column, which she wrote under the pen name Iola. She didn't stick to safe, neutral subjects in her journalism. Instead, Wells wrote about poverty in the black community and about the widespread oppression African Americans experienced.

The white establishment didn't care much for Wells's outspokenness. Eventually, the school district fired Wells in response to her criticism. It was unfair, but she refused to shut up. Just as it was her duty to care for her family when her parents died, Wells felt it was her duty to help care for her community, as well.

And there was an evil in her community that needed to be exposed. Racial tensions still high, whites often found excuses to murder people of color, especially black men. The whites made up reasons about why they had to do it—claiming that the black men had attacked white women or children.

In fact, the black men had done nothing except live and work in a deeply troubled society. These murders, called **lynchings**, became more and more common. Worse, they seemed to be entertainment for the whites who participated. People sold souvenir photos of various lynchings; they took pictures of themselves with the bodies to share with friends.

Incensed by the lynching of three friends in her community, Ida B. Wells risked her life and spoke up. Wells forced the subject into the spotlight. Many people, even some African Americans, wanted her to keep her voice down. That just wasn't in her nature. A black women's club raised money so she could dedicate herself to investigating the causes and effects of lynching.

Soon, she produced a pamphlet called *Southern Horrors: Lynch Law in All Its Phases*. It struck a nerve, revealing the racism behind these murders. It pointed out that many of the victims had done nothing more than succeed when whites had not. Many whites were so incensed by the pamphlet that they destroyed the newspaper where Wells worked. They also threatened to kill her.

At this point, it would have been safer for Wells to lower her voice. Instead, she raised it even more. Since she couldn't go home, she stayed on the road. Traveling the Northeast, she gave a lecture tour on lynching.

Everywhere she went, she talked about these terrible crimes. She would not let them go unmentioned. She would not let them go unchallenged.

For the rest of her life, Wells advocated for freedom, for equality, but most important, for the end of lynching in the United States. Though she could have slowed down, or quieted down, she never did.

She encouraged others to organize and to speak up. To stop the hideous legacy of lynching, she wrote, spoke, and protested at the top of her voice.

Only when she passed away in 1931 did Ida B. Wells rest. Her writings, however, survive. They still shout—still demand and expect change.

Wells may be quiet now, but she will *never* be silent.

Anna Maria Chávez

Anna Maria Chávez
1968–

It was graffiti on a cave wall that shaped the direction of Anna Maria Chávez's life.

As a Girl Scout in Arizona, Chávez had learned that it was important to protect the environment. She and her troop had visited lots of special places, including those with historical significance. Her Scout leader taught the girls to leave no trace of themselves behind. That way, each trail and monument would last, unharmed and ready for the next visitors to enjoy.

Chávez took that lesson to heart. When she was twelve, she went on vacation with her family, and they explored ancient caves with wonder. To Chávez, they were time machines. Thousand-year-old art from long-vanished Native Americans still decorated the caves. It was a beautiful link from the past to the present, one that inspired and moved her.

Then she found the graffiti.

She wasn't the only modern person to stand in those caves and look at the art. But some of the other modern people had decided to carelessly deface the walls. They had left more than a trace behind. They had nearly ruined an ancient wonder!

Furious, Chávez asked her mother how people could do such a thing. More important, how could she stop them in the future? She was sure there had to be a way to protect this precious part of our past.

Instead of stepping in and telling Chávez what to do, her mother helped her figure it out on her own. How would she go about protecting this cave? Considering it a moment, Chávez decided that there should be a law. Coaxing her along, her mother asked, "Who does that, Anna Maria?"

Chávez knew the answers: a lawyer.

At that moment, she decided that she would be a lawyer. Plowing through school, Chávez's passion never wavered. Our cultural past and how to protect it led her to graduate with a degree in American history from Yale. That was one piece of the goal. The next was to become someone who could also *protect* that heritage, so she attended law school in her home state of Arizona.

For many years, she worked as a lawyer for several government agencies. Soon, she realized that she could make an even bigger difference by reaching out to girls who were just like her. Spirited, passionate, intelligent girls—where better to find them than the Girl Scouts? The very same Scouts that had started Chávez on her path when she was twelve!

In 2011, the Girl Scouts of America chose Chávez to be their new chief executive officer. The first Latina to lead the organization, she also knew it was time to modernize the Girl Scouts. She became the link to the past, shoring up all the great things about the organization that had inspired her, and adding new programs for twenty-first-century girls.

To the program, she's added STEM (Science, Technology, Engineering, Math)–related activities to the Scouts. Joining with Sheryl Sandberg and LeanIn. org, Chávez is encouraging girls to ban the word *bossy*. Chávez knew from personal experience that there was a big difference between being "bossy" and being the boss.

And for her, it all started with the Girl Scouts— and one careless, unknown graffiti artist.

Sheryl Sandberg

Sheryl Sandberg
1969–

Sheryl Sandberg always expected to be part of a social movement. She says she expected to do that in a nonprofit organization—never in the corporate world.

But the corporate world is where Sandberg made a name for herself, and opened a path for other women to come after her. After earning degrees in finance from Harvard University, Sandberg worked her way to the top of Google—the company (that owns the search engine!).

Then she traded searching for poking. Taking a position as Facebook's first female chief officer of operations, Sandberg did something few professional women achieve. She became part of the C-level, one of the highest-ranking senior executives in the world.

It would have been easy for Sandberg to look out

only for herself. After all, she was struggling against the same preconceived notions about women in the workplace that any woman does.

People expected her to be quieter. They expected her to do less. They expected to pay her less, and thought she'd eventually leave work to be a stay-at-home parent.

So Sandberg had a choice. She could keep her head down and worry about her own career. Or instead, she could reach out to other women, and to young women, and even little girls—to help them get closer to their goals.

She started with advice for women already in the workplace. After giving a talk on this subject, Sandberg wrote a book called *Lean In*. (It became an international bestseller, by the way!)

In it, Sandberg talks about obstacles in the workplace for women. Sometimes, it's something women can control—like negotiating for a better salary. Sometimes, it's something to overcome, like being an effective leader when people think they don't like working for women.

That's an especially tricky one! The same qualities that people thought made men good leaders?

They thought it made women unpleasant. The B-word came up a lot. That's right, *bossy*.

Assertive boys demonstrate leadership qualities. Assertive girls? *Bossy*.

Sandberg's been called that too many times to count! But she knew the next generation of girls would have to keep climbing. So she formed a partnership with the Girl Scouts. They created a public awareness campaign called Ban Bossy.

Girls hear "Don't be bossy!" so often that by the time they reach middle school, they're way less likely to take a leadership position. They talk down their own achievements and doubt their own accomplishments.

Crazy, right? But it's true! That's why Sandberg, Anna Maria Chávez, and the Girl Scouts want to ban bossy. They want to encourage girls to speak up, to stand up. They want them to realize it is okay to know the answer. And it's really okay if they are sure!

Right now, Sandberg is part of the 17 percent of women who make up C-level executives. Eighty-three to seventeen—that's a pretty wide gap. With inspirational talks, books, and of course, banning bossy, Sandberg knows what she wants the world to look like for her generation of women—and yours.

"A truly equal world," she said in her book, "would be one where women ran half our countries and companies and men ran half our homes."

Not 83/17: 50/50, right down the middle. It's equal, it's fair, and Sheryl Sandberg knows it's *possible*.

MS. INDEPENDENCE

In 1912, Juliette Gordon Low founded the Girl Scouts of America. One of the most popular organizations for young women, the Girl Scouts teach independence, character and leadership. And yes, they sell cookies— seven hundred million dollars' worth every year.

Notable former Girl Scouts include astronauts Mae Jemison and Sally Ride, publishers Susan Taylor and Phoebe Eng, and First Ladies Michelle Obama, Nancy Reagan, Laura Bush, and Hillary Rodham Clinton.

But perhaps the most notable Girl Scout of all time is Jennifer Sharpe, from Detroit, Michigan. In 2008, this teen entrepreneur sold *17,328 boxes of cookies*!

Ellen DeGeneres

Ellen DeGeneres

1958–

When Ellen DeGeneres was a little girl, she had a plan.

"I wanted to be special, I wanted people to like me, I wanted to be famous," she said. Embracing the world in all its quirks, and finding happiness in its darkness became her trademark.

DeGeneres's first act as a comedian came when she was thirteen. Her parents had divorced, and her mother was suffering from cancer.

Discovering that she could distract her mother by making her laugh, DeGeneres took advantage of this secret superpower. To her, it was amazing that she could help someone have a better day just by being funny. Sometimes, she needed the funny to help herself get by, too.

After she graduated high school, DeGeneres moved to New Orleans to start her career. There, she met Kat Perkoff and they fell in love. They were a good match. Both creative, Perkoff urged DeGeneres to hone her comedy, and DeGeneres encouraged Perkoff to keep writing poetry. They didn't have a lot of money, but they had each other.

Then in 1980, Perkoff died in a car accident. DeGeneres was crushed. She couldn't stop thinking about death. She didn't understand how the fleas in her mattress were still alive but this wonderful person was not. How could these unimportant bugs that left welts on her arms still be around, while Kat was gone?

The question couldn't be answered. At least, no one on earth could answer it. DeGeneres kept rolling the questions over and over in her mind until they started to take form. They slowly became the questions she would ask in her first famous piece of stand-up comedy, "A Phone Call to God."

DeGeneres went on to be voted the Funniest Person in America. The first woman ever to be invited to sit with Johnny Carson on *The Tonight Show*, DeGeneres managed to make her childhood wish come true, bit by bit.

When she got her own television show, she felt like she'd almost made it. Almost.

Bravery wasn't part of her plan, but she needed it. Because she realized that if she wanted people to like *her*, then she would have to be herself. All the time— honestly and completely. So when she told the world she was gay in 1997, many people cheered. No one as famous as DeGeneres had ever admitted that before.

Other people, however, were upset with her honesty. There was a fierce debate in the media about DeGeneres, making her the butt of many cruel jokes.

Suddenly, she lost her job, her television show, and everything she'd worked so hard to create. She couldn't help but believe that people had never really liked her at all. For the next three years, DeGeneres struggled with that. Then she remembered that she had a superpower. She could make people laugh! So she set out to do just that.

Returning to her early comedy roots, she went on tour. Telling the same kind of stories she always had, only now honest about her whole life, she discovered that people welcomed her back fondly.

Shortly after the terrorist attacks on the United States on September 11, 2001, the whole country needed someone to distract them from sadness and despair. Never one to tell cruel jokes (she'd had too much experience being joked about!), DeGeneres was chosen to host the Emmy Awards.

Her appearance was a smash hit. She helped people laugh again in a very dark time. And slowly, she came back into the light. Instead of going back to sitcoms, she started her own daytime talk show— making people laugh every single day.

You probably know DeGeneres best as the voice of Dory from *Finding Nemo*. The screenwriter wrote that part especially for her. Dory's philosophy *Just keep swimming!* is a lot like DeGeneres's personal philosophy.

Even when it's hard, even when things are bad, you keep going and you keep laughing. Now, DeGeneres has the life she always wanted. She's famous, she's special—and people like her!

FIRSTS!

In 1815, Molly Williams became the first female firefighter in the United States. This was remarkable because she was a woman—but also because she was enslaved. Owned by a New York merchant, Williams nonetheless joined Oceanus Engine Company. Known as Volunteer #11, Williams served tirelessly through blizzards, influenza epidemics, and of course, many, many fires.

Etta James

Etta James
1938–2012

In spite of a hard life, or possibly because of it, Etta James helped shape the sound of R & B, soul and blues music for decades.

Generations of young musical artists, including Janis Joplin, Diana Ross, Christina Aguilera, Beyoncé, and Adele took their inspiration from James. What's interesting is that James was legendary for her rich and raucous singing—but she hated it when people forced her to sing.

James's mother was only fourteen when she had her, and her father was nowhere to be found. Unfortunately, her stepfather could be found down the hall, usually drinking and gambling. In the middle of the night, he'd wake up a six-year-old James to sing for his friends. If she refused, he beat her.

James found her solace in singing for herself, and in the church. She could make her voice soar, and fly away with it. Radio stations played her songs; they called her a prodigy—and she was. She wasn't even ten years old yet!

Eventually, her foster parents—the ones who were supposed to protect her—decided to use her talent to get rich. When they demanded that the church start paying James for her singing, she was no longer invited to perform there.

When she was twelve, she moved to San Francisco and started working for Johnny Otis, a famous bandleader. At first, he insisted that James sing in a group. People couldn't help but notice, though, that James stood out. With her platinum-blond hair and a big, beautiful voice, it was obvious she was meant to be a star.

After performing her first solo single with Otis's band, James produced her first solo record at the age of sixteen. Her hit music was a skillful blend of gospel, R & B, and blues. Though she had many hits, "At Last" became her biggest and her signature song.

Though the music was good, life was still tough for James. Struggling to get by on her own, she started abusing drugs. As her addiction grew, her career and her income slipped away. Things got so desperate that once she stole her band's instruments to pay for more drugs.

This decline lasted until she was arrested on drug charges. The judge sent her to rehab instead of to jail. After long, hard months and years of rehabilitation, James finally beat her addictions at the age of fifty. Ashamed of the way she'd behaved as an addict, James was determined to start again.

Refreshed and renewed, James threw herself back into her music. Before, she'd had hit songs but wasn't very famous. Too erratic and unreliable on drugs, James found that when she was sober, she was focused. Putting all her energy into music, James started to get the recognition as an artist that she deserved.

After decades of singing hit songs, James was inducted into the Rock and Roll Hall of Fame and the Blues Hall of Fame. She got a star on the Hollywood Walk of Fame, and she won Grammy after Grammy for her brand-new music.

Named one of the greatest singers of all time by *Rolling Stone* magazine, Etta James continued to perform into her seventies.

But you know what? She still never sang unless she wanted to. Her son Donto reported that she'd make up her mind about a performance on the morning that she was supposed to appear.

Music was James's gift, and she alone decided when she would share it!

FIRSTS!

Many people say that women earned the right to vote in the United States in 1920, but that's not *entirely* true. Though the 19th Amendment to the Constitution affirmed the right of any citizen to vote, regardless of gender, there were other laws that kept many women (and men) from the ballot box. For example, Native Americans weren't considered citizens until 1924—they weren't allowed to vote until then. Chinese-Americans were denied **suffrage** until 1943; Japanese-Americans, 1952. African Americans' right to vote wasn't fully recognized until 1965. So when people celebrate women's suffrage, it's important to remember— not all women, not all at one time!

Aishwarya Rai Bachchan

Aishwarya Rai Bachchan

1973–

Born in Mumbai, India, Aishwarya Rai Bachchan always stood out. Captivating everyone around her with her striking green eyes, Bachchan started modeling in ninth grade.

At the same time, she attended prestigious schools. In high school, she loved zoology, so she planned to be a physician. That didn't quite work out for her, so she changed her path. This time, she decided to pursue a career in architecture.

She entered the Raheja College of Arts to study for this new path. Then one of her friends talked her into entering the Ford Supermodel Contest. Bachchan was the only one who was shocked when she won!

This vaulted her into the Miss World pageant, where it all came back to her eyes. During the contest, the judges asked her how she would leave her mark on history. Completely unexpected, the answer resonated with the audience.

"I will leave my eyes to an eye bank," she said, "so that someone can see the wonder of this world through my eyes long after I am gone."

It was a real departure from the other contestants' answers. In India, fewer than 5 percent of all people donate their eyes. And doctors are able to use only about 15 percent of those donations. There was a real need to raise awareness, and Bachchan did it in a single sentence.

Bachchan won the Miss World pageant in 1994, and became a spokesperson for the Eye Bank Association of India. She had to take off a year of school to fulfill her duties.

Traveling all over the world, she spoke about eye donation and the importance of helping the needy. After that, instead of hitting the books, she hit the small screen in television commercials.

In just thirty seconds, Bachchan dazzled viewers everywhere. That's right—she got famous from TV commercials! The major directors in India's **Bollywood** film industry couldn't wait to hire her.

Soon she landed her first film role. In *Iruvar*, she played two different characters. A huge success, the film (and Bachchan) won critical acclaim in festivals around the world.

A long way from architecture, Bachchan took her career turn into acting very seriously. Just one year later, she starred in *Jeans*—the only movie that India submitted to the Academy Awards in the United States for consideration.

As Bachchan's fame spread, she found that she could lend her voice (and eyes!) to the causes that mattered the most to her. Not only did she continue to advocate for cornea donation, she also stepped up as the Goodwill Ambassador of Smile Train, a program that provides children in need with surgery to repair cleft lips and palates.

Though Bachchan became neither doctor nor architect, education remains important to her. She speaks out for the rights of girls to get a full education. It's her belief that all girls everywhere need the opportunity to decide their own fate, including in her native India.

After all, Bachchan didn't choose to have dazzling eyes. That was a quirk of fate. But she *could* choose her career. She *did* choose her path. Now that she's the most famous Bollywood actor in the world, it would be easy to disappear into luxury.

Instead, Aishwarya Rai Bachchan sees herself helping others every single day. For her, it definitely sounds like the eyes have it!

MAD, BAD, AND DANGEROUS TO KNOW

Say you were a Roman empress with a big problem: your husband is keeping your baby boy from becoming the next emperor. Do you convince him to step down?

Nope, you hire Locusta—a poisoner so famous, she ran a school to teach other women her deadly tricks! Getting her start in Gaul (now France), Locusta worked her way to Rome with her devilish decoctions. She was just what the empress ordered when Agrippina decided her husband Claudius had to go.

Locusta prepared a poisonous **repast** of mushrooms for Claudius. They only made him sick, perhaps a miscalculation on Locusta's part. Or maybe not. She also poisoned the feather that Claudius used to try to make himself throw up.

In no time, the old emperor was dead as a doornail. And the new one? Was hiring Locusta to get rid of his stepbrother. You can't keep a good poisoner down!

Estée Lauder

Estée Lauder
1906–2004

Though you probably recognize the name Estée Lauder, you may think it just belongs to a cosmetics company. Actually, the cosmetics company was named after the woman!

As a child, Lauder worked alongside her father in his hardware store. This gave her valuable market training and sharpened her business **acumen**. Then as a teen, she started selling her uncle's face creams door-to-door.

During one of those sales visits, the young Lauder found herself in a glamorous spa. Surrounded by elegance and beauty, she was taken by one of the patron's gorgeous silk shirt. Working up her nerve, Lauder approached the woman and asked her where she bought it.

With a sniff, the woman looked her over, then replied, "What difference could it possibly make? You could never afford it."

Shocked, Lauder hurried away. Embarrassed by the slight, she swore to herself that no one would snub her like that ever again. She would make so much money, she would be able to buy anything she wanted.

Building on her uncle's formulas, Lauder started to create face creams, perfumes, and cosmetics of her own. Instead of building a store to sell them, she convinced department stores to open a makeup counter.

The makeup counters were tiny spas, right in the middle of some of the most prestigious stores in the world. Brightly lit, staffed with knowledgeable people, the Estée Lauder counter became a destination.

To encourage people to try her products, she let them sample them, right there in the store. And to reward loyal customers, she always included a free gift with every purchase (usually a lipstick!).

Soon, Lauder had makeup counters all over the *world*. She made an especially big splash when she came out with a bath oil called Youth-Dew. It replaced perfume, and it was a hit.

Other perfumes followed, along with unscented cosmetics, men's products and more.

From a merchant's daughter to the CEO of a five *billion* dollar corporation bearing her name, Estée Lauder more than fulfilled her promise to herself.

Not only had she become wealthy, she'd become one of the richest women in the United States. And it all started with a rude stranger in a pretty shirt. How about that?

Shirley Chisholm

Shirley Chisholm

1924–2005

It's easy for powerful people to get the government to listen to them. It's a lot harder for everyone else—which is why Shirley Chisholm decided to go into politics.

The first black woman elected to Congress, Chisholm spoke up for the underprivileged and underserved. She knew a lot about struggling. Growing up in the New York neighborhood of Bedford-Stuyvesant, Chisholm experienced the Great Depression firsthand.

Her mother cleaned houses, and her father worked in a factory—and with four daughters making a family of six, things were pretty tough for them. As a black family before the civil rights movement, they also learned about discrimination and prejudice.

That meant when Chisholm got to Congress, she refused to play politics. Instead, she was there to make changes for people like her family, and the families who voted for her in Bed-Stuy.

That meant she refused an assignment to the Agriculture Committee. What did that have to do with the city people who had elected her? Nothing!

The other representatives were shocked. That's not how things were supposed to work. They expected Chisholm to meekly accept any assignment and to be grateful for it. After all, she was a woman. And black. And a first timer!

So what? That didn't make the lousy assignment any better! Chisholm continued her protest. Eventually, the Speaker of the House moved her to Veteran Affairs—something very relevant to the young men in her district. They were, after all, being sent to fight a war in Vietnam.

Chisholm protested that war, too. Why were they sending young men to die in a fight for someone else's land, when there were people starving, suffering and needful back at home? She refused to vote yes to any bill that granted more money to the war effort.

Instead, she focused on the rights of women and

children, and for people to make a better living wage. She fought for better child care, and to create food programs for the poor. When she hired staff for her office, she made sure all of them were women, and half of them were black.

Education was also important to Chisholm. She started her career as a teacher and, as a congress-woman, campaigned for school lunch programs and other education bills.

Being the first black woman elected to Congress wasn't Chisholm's only first. In 1972, she was the first black woman to run for president of the United States, as well. Her campaign buttons read MISS CHIS FOR PRES! And FOLLOW THE CHISHOLM TRAIL TO 1600 PENNSYLVANIA STREET.

Not everyone was excited about this. During her campaign, Chisholm survived three separate **assassination** attempts. Then she shocked people by visiting her opponent in the hospital after he survived *his* assassination attempt.

It didn't matter that they didn't share the same politics, though. What mattered to Chisholm was that he was a human being, and was suffering.

With Shirley Chisholm, people always came first.

That's why she served in the House of Representatives for fourteen years—and that's why she called herself Fighting Shirley Chisholm.

She wasn't there to make friends. She was there to make a difference!

FIRSTS!

The first woman to run for president of the United States was Victoria Claflin Woodhull. A suffragette and outspoken activist, Woodhull accepted the nomination from the Equal Rights Party in 1872. (Unfortunately, few people in the government took her seriously. They threw most of her votes away.)

Audra McDonald

Audra McDonald

1970–

From the very start, Audra McDonald was destined to make music her life.

Her father was stationed in West Berlin when McDonald was born; the family soon retired to Fresno, California. In elementary school, McDonald sang and acted in local theaters—her sister Alison joined her there.

They had come by the musical talent honestly. Both of their parents were musical, and their aunts performed in a gospel group they called the McDonald Sisters.

Music tugged McDonald along. It came to her naturally, easily. She loved disappearing into a role or a song. This led her to enroll in a performing arts high school. From there, she went to the acclaimed fine arts college, Juilliard.

There, for the first time, she had trouble with her music.

Not the music exactly. McDonald's voice was so strong and so soaring, her teachers tried to push her toward classical and opera. She excelled at it and trained in classical voice under the famous soprano Ellen Faull.

The thing was, while McDonald loved all kinds of music, she felt most at home doing musical theater. She preferred contemporary music; it seemed like the best fit for her. It was hard, with her heart telling her one thing and her esteemed professors telling her something else.

While still in college, she won a part in the chorus of the Broadway production of *The Secret Garden*. Juilliard encouraged her to audition and let her take time off from her schooling to be part of the show.

McDonald cleared her mind while on tour with that cast. Her work there gave her professors and mentors the opportunity to see that's where she fit best.

Finally, everyone agreed that McDonald found her place. She did belong on the Broadway stages. She was a fantastic singer and actor. And she proved that by winning her first Tony Award for her role in *Carousel*.

Her first. She's won five more since then—the only person in the world to win so many! She earned three of them before the age of thirty. No one else has ever done that, either!

Even though her heart belongs to music first, McDonald also loves acting. She's appeared on television and in films. She has also been praised for her turns in Shakespeare's *Twelfth Night* and Lorraine Hansberry's *A Raisin in the Sun*.

Audra McDonald never doubted that she had talent. No one else doubted it, either. That didn't mean her rise to stardom was easy. In fact, it was pretty hard, with her teachers pushing her one way while she longed to go another.

In the end, she listened to her heart, and now she makes beautiful music every day of the year!

Murasaki Shikibu

Murasaki Shikibu
c. 978–1014/1025

Unlike the other fabulous ladies in this book, Murasaki Shikibu's real name remains a mystery.

This clever girl who grew up in Japan's Heian Period was raised by her father, a scholar and a governor. He allowed her to learn Chinese (usually forbidden to girls) and encouraged her intellectual curiosity. She was such a good student that her father lamented that if she had only been a boy, everything would have been perfect.

If this hurt Murasaki's feelings, we'll never know. What we do know is that she was selected to become one of Empress Akiko's ladies-in-waiting. Moving to the Imperial Court, Murasaki's given name went unrecorded. She lived and died in anonymity, the date of her death unknown for certain. This was common of the women of the time.

She, however, preserved much of the court's drama—allowing us to take a peek a thousand years into the past even today. How? Murasaki kept a diary! Copies of it still exist today, a day-by-day window into an otherwise hidden court.

During the same time, she wrote the world's first novel, *The Tale of Genji*. It was about a golden prince, and—surprise!—his life in a court full of intrigue! Murasaki didn't have to go far for inspiration.

But she went a great deal further than anyone else ever had. Crafting fifty-four chapters, she produced a novel that captured all the pomp, glory, and desperation found in the Imperial Court. The book was an instant hit.

The original manuscript is missing, but a later scroll containing the Golden Prince's story survives. It also gives its author half of her name.

Her true name is unknown. Some historians think it might have been Fujiwara Takako. Others aren't so sure. Women were absorbed into the court at the time, obscuring their identities. So when it came time to credit *The Tale of Genji*, Shikibu simply described her father's job. No identity for herself, there! But

Murasaki—ah, that's the name of her novel's heroine. The ladies at court decided to call the author that, too.

We know Murasaki Shikibu's name because she wrote the world's first novel—and because she wrote the world's first novel, she has a name!

Elizabeth Blackwell

Elizabeth Blackwell

1821–1910

The first woman with a medical degree in the United States, Elizabeth Blackwell believed that *all* good ideas were achievable. Her own remarkable career is proof of that.

Much more interested in metaphysics than science, Blackwell went into teaching first. With a love of history, and a community that believed that teaching was one of the few jobs suitable for women, Blackwell seemed to be a perfect fit.

In fact, it made her sick to her stomach to look at medical books; even thinking about the human body in parts was too much. History and teaching were much more to her liking!

Then a close family friend fell ill with uterine cancer. Medical treatment wasn't as advanced in the

1800s as it is now. Worse, male doctors often had little sympathy for female patients, especially if they were suffering from a disease that specifically targeted women.

As she was dying, Blackwell's friend told her that she would have suffered less if she'd had a female doctor. Something about that idea stuck in Blackwell's brain. She couldn't stop thinking about it. Why couldn't women have a female doctor? After all, they understood women's bodies quite well!

The reason was that medical schools at the time didn't admit women as students. Women were expected to nurse their children at home, or perhaps become a nurse in the hospital. Surgery and medical practice were permitted for men alone. They didn't even think women were smart enough to pass the classes.

So Blackwell studied with doctors for a year to get ready to apply for medical school. Though she had many allies and friends in her private life, she didn't have many in the medical community. The men there discouraged her. Turn back now, they told her. This is no place for you.

Those who didn't discourage her had unusual

advice. Some suggested that she go to Paris to study, where the doctors might be more welcoming of a female student. Or, another suggested, she should disguise herself as a man and sneak into school!

Instead, Blackwell applied to as many schools as she could, as herself. She had no intention of tricking anyone. When she became a doctor—and she was sure it would be when, not if—it would be as herself, 100 percent.

When she applied to Geneva Medical College in New York, the dean put her admission up to a vote. The 150 male medical students got to decide whether they would let Blackwell study with them. They were so full of themselves, they all voted yes, as a joke. They didn't think Blackwell had the smarts to keep up.

They thought wrong. Blackwell flew through her classes. Even when some professors tried to exclude her, she fought to be included. Graduating in 1849, she was the first woman in the United States to earn a medical degree.

That wasn't enough, though. She continued her studies in Europe, becoming the first female doctor of record in Britain, as well. Because it had been so hard for her to pursue her career as a doctor, she started mentoring other young women who wanted to follow the same path.

It was true for her, and it was true for them: if it was a good idea for women to go into medicine, it was possible to make it happen. Blackwell knew that she *could* become a doctor, so she refused to stop until she *did*.

HARD-CORE BATTLE QUEENS

One of the most revered warriors of the Chiricahua Apache was named Lozen. As a child, she chose to become a shaman and a warrior. Fighting alongside her brother Victorio, Lozen was his right-hand woman, second-in-command and "shield to her people" throughout the late 1800s.

She once led a whole village safely across the Rio Grande, then dashed back to the battle on the other side of the raging waters. After her brother died, Lozen joined Geronimo to fight the last campaign of the Apache Wars.

Billie Jean King

Billie Jean King

1943–

Imagine you're one of the biggest tennis stars in the *world*. Imagine you started winning Grand Slam titles at the age of fifteen, and you're at the top of the game.

Now imagine that the boy on the court next to you is going to win fifteen thousand dollars more for the exact same competition. Stinks, huh?

It happened to Billie Jean King. She started playing professional tennis in 1961. Winning her way straight to the top, King was the number one female tennis player in the world by 1966. And by then she was already vocal about how differently female athletes were being treated than male athletes.

The unfair differences in prize money were one big issue. The other was the way female players were treated. Women had to wear short white skirts. Rather than treating these young women as the athletes they were, many treated them like novelties. Girls weren't expected to be active and athletic, so people discriminated against them.

King joined a new women's tennis tour, and raised eyebrows. Was she some kind of activist? Some kind of radical? Well, a little bit, she definitely was. She'd started playing tennis on public courts. Everything was fair and equal there; she wanted professional courts to be fair and equal, too.

Forming the Women's Tennis Association in 1973, King really started to roar. She informed the U.S. Open committee that unless they equalized the prize money for men and women, she wouldn't play. And neither would any of the other female players.

It was a bold move. The U.S. Open agreed, becoming the first tennis competition with equalized prizes.

King wasn't done, however. To bring more visibility, she founded *WomenSports* magazine, then the Women's Sports Foundation, *then* World Team Tennis.

Now, instead of playing the game exclusively,

King spent much of her time advocating for equality for female athletes.

Of course, when you speak so loudly, a lot of people listen. That includes people who disagree with you.

A former tennis player and Wimbledon champion, Bobby Riggs decided to prove once and for all that women weren't as good as men at the game. He challenged Margaret Court on Mother's Day, 1973—and won. Next, he aimed for King.

At first, she refused his challenge. She didn't have anything to prove—and he expected her to play for free! Then people raised one hundred thousand dollars in prize money for the Battle of the Sexes: Billie Jean King versus Bobby Riggs, in Houston's Astrodome.

This time, King agreed. She was nervous, of course. She was afraid that if she lost, it would ruin all the hard work she'd put into helping tennis become an equal-opportunity sport.

When she stepped onto the court, though, there was nothing to worry about. Running Bobby Riggs to exhaustion, King beat him handily in all three sets.

If anyone doubted just how important this match was—more than fifty million people watched, eager for the outcome. An article in *The New York Times* declared, "She convinced skeptics that a female athlete can survive pressure-filled situations and that men are as susceptible to nerves as women."

Obviously! Billie Jean King had been saying the same thing for years. Now that she'd won the Battle of the Sexes, the world had to listen!

MS. INDEPENDENCE

Charlotte "Charley" Parkhurst was one of the greatest stagecoach drivers in the American Old West. Short, strong, and willful, Parkhurst worked as a stable *boy* and learned to drive the coaches.

In men's clothing, Parkhurst went on to Georgia and California, where she earned her living as a driver—moving on only when her secret identity was threatened.

It wasn't until she died that people learned her true identity. Dressing as a man gave Parkhurst the freedom to come and go as she pleased, the right to have a career, and the right to vote. It didn't, however, stop her from giving birth to a child at some point during her life!

Hatshepsut

Hatshepsut

1508 BCE—1458 BCE

Egypt has had many queens but only one female pharaoh: Hatshepsut (hat-SHEP-suht).

Her name literally means "foremost of noble women." If she'd been a boy, Hatshepsut would have been the heir to the throne when her father died. Instead, her stepson, Tuthmosis (tut-MO-sis) III, was crowned.

That didn't work for Hatshepsut.

Wasn't she the eldest child of the last pharaoh? Didn't she, too, carry the blood of the gods in her veins? Yes, and yes! So why did she have to step aside?

Hatshepsut decided she wouldn't. Taking the crown as **regent**, she transformed herself into the pharaoh. Dressing in men's clothing, she put on the pharaoh's ceremonial beard. And she didn't just dress the part.

Like all pharaohs, she built temples and statues in her own honor. One still stands today at Deir el-Bahri. This was the temple where she emphasized that she was a daughter of the sun god Amun. That was her lineage after all—very important to the Egyptians.

Like any pharaoh, she led her country's army in battle. She sent scientists out to search the world and bring her wonders. And she built more temples, statues, and monuments than almost any other pharaoh (aside from the construction-happy Rameses II, that is!).

For twenty-two years, Hatshepsut ruled her people in peace and prosperity. Some scholars think she groomed her daughter Neferure to succeed her. Which probably would have worked—she was the eldest daughter of the pharaoh after all.

But Tuthmosis III was grown now, and he thought he'd waited long enough to rule. He took the throne, and Hatshepsut's daughter disappeared from history. He wasn't yet satisfied. To strengthen his own reign, he decided he needed to erase Hatshepsut's completely.

They Did What?

He sent people out to destroy her name and her image everywhere it could be found. With chisels and hammers, Tuthmosis III's lackeys literally stripped Hatshepsut's legacy from the walls of her own temples.

Hatshepsut faded from history, almost forgotten.

Except, modern archaeologists grew curious. Who was this figure who had been chipped away from the temple walls? Why would someone go to that much trouble? They scoured the monuments until they found an answer.

Now we know Hatshepsut as one of Egypt's most prolific pharaohs. In his attempt to erase her, Tuthmosis III memorialized her better than she had herself. That's probably not how he expected his plan to work!

HARD-CORE BATTLE QUEENS

In southern Britain, 60 AD, Romans broke their **treaty** with the local Celtic government. Since the king had recently died, they figured his widow, Queen Boudicca, for an easy target and attacked. Bad idea.

In revolt, Boudicca raised a hundred thousand soldiers and went to war. She destroyed three cities, including London, and wiped out ten thousand troops from the world's finest military in the process!

HARD-CORE BATTLE QUEENS

In 1900, Britain decided to invade the Ashanti Empire in eastern Africa. (They apparently forgot Boudicca's lesson!) The colonialists exiled the Asante king and demanded their queen, Yaa Asantewaa, give up the golden throne. She refused.

When the men of her community considered surrender, she refused that, too. She fired a gun in the air and declared, "I shall call upon my fellow women. We will fight! We will fight till the last of us falls in the battlefields!" And they did, until Asantewaa was captured and exiled in 1902.

Edmonia Lewis

Edmonia Lewis

c. 1844–1907

When sculptor Edmonia Lewis was a little girl, her family called her Wildfire.

The daughter of a freed black man and an Ojibwe (Chippewa) woman, Lewis spent most of her childhood traveling with her aunts' tribe in upstate New York.

It's possible she may have never discovered her artistic talent, if a successful half brother hadn't helped her get into Oberlin College. There, she changed her name to Mary Edmonia. She thought that was better suited to college than Wildfire.

Oberlin was a center of **abolitionist** thought. The people there ardently fought against human slavery in the United States. This appealed to Lewis for deeply personal reasons. It also made it possible for this black, **indigenous** woman to attend college at all.

At first, she studied literature. Soon, though, she realized she had a real talent for art—especially drawing. Excelling in art class after art class, Lewis blossomed. Unfortunately, Oberlin had good abolitionist intentions—but flawed, imperfect people.

Bullied and insulted, Lewis struggled to find a place among her classmates. It didn't matter what she did. Her colleagues and contemporaries refused to treat her as an equal.

In fact, in an attempt to push Lewis out of school, they falsely accused her of poisoning two white students. An angry mob sought her out. They beat her viciously.

Wrongly accused, Lewis had to recover on her own. By the time the false charges against her were dropped, Lewis's career at Oberlin was officially over. She moved to Boston to get a new start.

There, she met a sculptor named Edward A. Brackett. He taught Lewis how to sculpt, and soon she built her own studio.

Selling portraits of famous abolitionists gave Lewis a measure of success and financial security.

One of her sculptures sold so well that she earned enough money to travel to Rome.

Rome! Home of ancient sculpture and modern thought! Many Americans had moved to the Italian capital, **expatriates** in search of lives full of art and culture. Lewis joined them. Her talent set her apart, and so did her subject matter.

Alternating between religious, abolitionist, and indigenous themes, Lewis didn't spend her time sculpting dusty old busts of emperors and princes.

Instead, she created great works of art that protested slavery and celebrated her life as a free woman among the Ojibwe people. She also dug into history for inspiration. Her most famous work is a two-ton sculpture titled *The Death of Cleopatra.*

This sculpture brought her immense fame, but it was bittersweet. After exhibiting *The Death of Cleopatra* in the United States, Lewis had to return to Rome without it. She just couldn't afford the shipping charges.

Lewis continued sculpting and exhibiting art until she died. Her personal life in Italy is a mystery. She kept to herself and dedicated herself completely to her art. The first black and native sculptor managed to disappear into Rome, then fade from history.

But not completely. A cornerstone of American art history, Lewis stands out as someone who made art celebrating black and indigenous themes in an unjust time. It just goes to show that a Wildfire may dim, but it never goes out!

MAD, BAD, AND DANGEROUS TO KNOW

"Stagecoach" Mary Fields made her mark on the American Old West in the 1880s. This six-foot-tall African American woman picked fights, drank whiskey, smoked cigars—and delivered the mail! One of the very first mail coach drivers, Stagecoach Mary became a legend.

Once, after her coach got stuck in the snow, she hiked ten miles to deliver the mail. She also got into a shootout with a man who complained that she made more money than he did. Since we know about Stagecoach Mary, and that fella remains nameless, I think we know who won!

Suze Orman

Suze Orman
1951–

Suze Orman's first dream didn't come true.

In her first conversation with her college guidance counselor, Orman told him she wanted to be a brain surgeon. The counselor took one look at Orman's grades and told her to aim lower. Orman had a speech **impediment**. She couldn't pronounce her Rs, Ss, or Ts—which made it hard for her to read. When most kids are sounding words out, they learn to put sounds together with letters. This helps them eventually work through longer, more complicated words without assistance. Because Orman's speech didn't match the words on the page, she struggled with her reading.

Though she'd made it through high school and into the University of Illinois at Urbana-Champaign, she had to decide on a whole new course for herself on the first day. Because she thought it would be easy, Orman decided to major in social work.

Her speech and reading impediments flared up again in college. She had everything she needed to graduate, except for a foreign language class. She had enough trouble with English!

So Orman dropped out, one class shy of her degree. Buying a cheap van, she and some friends drove to California, where she ended up working as a waitress. Three years after dropping out, she worked up the nerve to take Spanish at Hayward State and finally earned her degree.

But by now, Orman knew she didn't want to become a social worker. That was her fallback idea. Instead, she wanted to open a restaurant. She enjoyed working with customers at the Buttercup Bakery, and the atmosphere made her happy. The more she thought about owning her own restaurant, the more excited she got.

One of the customers found out she was saving to open her own place. He donated two thousand dollars to her restaurant fund. Plus, he convinced other regular customers to donate as well. Fifty thousand dollars later, Orman was sitting in a broker's office, investing her money and planning to hire an architect.

Unfortunately, this second dream wouldn't come true, either. Her financial manager risked her money and lost it all. Now, Orman had only her salary as a waitress, no restaurant, and no way to pay back all those customers who had raised funds to help her.

She started studying finance carefully. Reading financial papers and following stock prices, she realized there was no reason why *she* couldn't become a broker. Getting an interview at a major stockbroker firm, she talked to five men in a single day. And most of them were pretty sure she couldn't do the job because she was a woman.

In fact, one of the managers believed that women didn't belong in the workplace. They should be at home, having babies and taking care of them. Orman asked him how much he planned to pay her to have babies.

To Orman's surprise, he hired her. (He hedged his bets, though. Six months or less—that's how long he told her she would last.) To this day, Orman believes she initially got the job because they wanted to fill a quota of female workers. Quota or not, she became one of their top brokers.

As she learned more about the finance industry,

she realized that her original broker had done something illegal with her money. That led Orman to sue the same company she worked for! Eventually, the company settled with her: they paid back all the money Orman's broker lost, and then some.

Now able to repay all the customers who'd put their faith in her, Orman realized her dreams had changed. She didn't want anyone else to lose their money in bad investments. In fact, she wanted to help people make good ones. Her new passion was empowering people with financial information.

To that end, she wrote several books. They all became bestsellers—and now Orman appears on her own television show, as well as others', as a financial adviser. She can reach out to millions with one appearance, educating her audience before they make the same financial mistakes she once did.

Her first dream didn't come true because she didn't believe in herself. Then her second dream fell through because she didn't know enough to help herself.

Now Suze Orman is a multimillionaire who spends every day helping people just like her make the right decisions with their money. It looks like the third time is the charm!

MAD, BAD, AND DANGEROUS TO KNOW

If you were a teenaged girl in seventeenth-century Hungary, it was in your best interest to move as far away from Csejte Castle as possible. The Countess Erzsébet Báthory lived there, and she had hideous taste in entertainment. She liked to torture people.

She would hire young women from the local countryside to come work in her castle. Then she'd pluck them off, one by one. She murdered at least eighty young women.

People claimed that the pursuit of eternal youth was the reason Erzsébet Báthory chose to kill young girls. By the time she was arrested, the stories claimed that she bathed in the girls' blood to keep her skin looking fresh and dewy.

Chances are, she didn't look so hot after she was **immured** (held prisoner) in a series of rooms in Csejte Castle. Four years later, she died there—alone. Her fate was much kinder than the ones she dealt to her victims.

Olga of Kiev

Olga of Kiev
c. 890–969

Born a Varyag—better known to you as a Viking—Princess Olga married Prince Igor of Kievan Rus (now Russia) when she was just thirteen. Leaving her home of Pskov behind, she endeared herself to her new subjects first as their princess, then as their queen.

Fierce and decisive, she took control of Kiev when a rival empire, the Drevlians of Polesia, murdered Igor. Olga became Kiev's **regent**. She would make decisions for her toddler son Prince Svyatoslav, until he was old enough to rule.

As far as the Drevlians were concerned, this young widow couldn't protect Kiev. They thought the Drevlian Prince Mal should step in. They sent twenty ambassadors to force Olga to marry him.

Big mistake.

With full control of the Rus Army, Olga captured the twenty unfortunate matchmakers and buried them alive. Then she sent a message to Polesia, telling them to send better representatives with their request next time.

Foolishly, the Drevlians complied. When the next batch of ambassadors arrived, Olga was ready to greet them in her own special way. She offered them a hot bath after their long ride. They accepted, and Olga locked them in a building and set it on fire.

After that, you'd think the Drevlians would have steered clear of Olga and her invitations. You'd be wrong. As a peace offering, she invited the Drevlian leaders and their soldiers to her husband's funeral.

A good host, Olga served plenty of wine and beer to her guests. Once they were drunk, she set her soldiers on them. On her command, they slaughtered an army of five thousand, and Olga wasn't done yet.

Perhaps bored by the gullible Drevlians, Olga decided on one last encounter with them. Instead of asking them to visit again, she gathered her army and went to their native Polesia to collect tributes. Outside each town, she massed her army. Then she sent word to the town's mayor. Surrender now, and survive. Terrified of the alternative, most towns gave in immediately (and were spared destruction!).

Unfortunately, the Drevlians of Iskorosten decided to resist Olga's invasion. Apparently, they didn't realize that Olga would ask for surrender only *once*. When Iskorosten refused to give her a tribute, Olga gave the signal.

She and her great army besieged the city. They swept through the town like locusts, obliterating everything in their path. It was just too much—Iskorosten finally surrendered. Now assured of her victory, Olga asked for a tribute once again. This time, all she wanted was one dove from each family.

A sweet symbol of peace? Not even a little. She and her men tied lit papers to the legs of each bird. Then they released them to fly back home. Iskorosten burned to the ground.

After that, the Drevlians didn't want Olga of Kiev to marry their prince anymore.

Satisfied, she returned home and continued her rule even after Prince Svyatoslav came of age. Unquestionably, her son knew that Kiev was safe in her hands. He left her in charge while he rode out with the Rus army to fortify and expand their borders.

After sixty-five years as Kiev's regent, Olga died as she ruled: in a city siege. But that wasn't the last of her, not quite. Almost six hundred years after her death, the Orthodox church **beatified** her and declared her equal to the apostles.

Viking princess, warrior queen, beloved saint— Olga of Kiev left an indelible mark on seven *hundred* years of Russian history.

MS. INDEPENDENCE

We haven't yet achieved our first interplanetary space mission, but when we do, we'll have Mary G. Ross to thank. A Native American scientist and mathematician, Ross worked for aerospace company Lockheed Martin. She was part of the Skunk Works.

No, that had nothing to do with smelly animals. It was the code name for their secret Advanced Development Program. Ross spent her time working out the details of interplanetary travel—how it would work, and how to achieve it with astronauts onboard.

Still top secret, most of Ross's work remains a mystery to the world at large. However, we have hints of her legacy as a founder of our future in space. A really big clue? She's one of the authors of the *NASA Planetary Flight Handbook Vol. III*!

Anna May Wong

Anna May Wong
(Wong Liu Tsong)
1905–1961

A third-generation Chinese American, Anna May Wong knew exactly what she wanted to be when she grew up: a movie star.

Wong was obsessed with movies before there *were* movies. She'd skip school and spend her lunch money at nickelodeon theaters. A nickelodeon worked a lot like a flip-book. Instead of films, it spun a series of photographs taken in order. When the cards flipped, the pictures moved—and Wong couldn't get enough of these five-cent dramas.

Growing up in sunny California, Wong watched the movie industry spring up around her. As nickelodeons gave way to silent films, it wasn't unusual to see movie cameras in any Los Angeles neighborhood. Whenever she found herself near a set,

Wong would beg to be added to the cast.

Wong's first big break was really more of a tiny crack, and it came when she was just fourteen years old. A friend got her a part as one of three hundred extras. She, like the other 299 girls cast, carried a lantern in the background. Way in the background. It was hardly a starring role, but so what? It was a role!

From that opportunity, Wong made sure she got herself hired as an extra as often as she could. She had the perfect flapper look—bobbed hair, round cheeks, sassy smile. It was hard to keep up with high school classes *and* a burgeoning movie career. So Wong did what she thought she had to: she dropped out of school.

She figured she was young enough to fail as an actress. She would give herself ten years to make it, and if she failed, she promised herself (and her family) that she would go back to school. There was no way she was going to let herself fail, though. Movies were Wong's life.

At the age of seventeen, she landed her first lead role. It was in a movie based on the opera *Madame Butterfly*, and she wowed audiences. Critics loved her. They couldn't stop talking about her brilliant performance and mesmerizing screen presence.

With this performance, Wong became the first Asian American woman to play the lead role in a Hollywood film. The problem was, like much of the United States at the time, Hollywood had a problem with actors of color. Directors usually cast white actors in Asian roles. It would have been shocking (and in some places, illegal) to cast her in a romantic role against a white actor.

This kept Wong from some of the best parts in Hollywood. Always a supporting character, directors plugged her into any role of color they could. During her career, Wong played American Indians, and Inuit Eskimos—and, of course, Asians of all kinds, as long as they weren't the star.

Wong wanted the romantic leads. She wanted to star in action serials. In short, she wanted the same opportunity that white actors had. Though she had achieved stardom in her first ten years of acting, it was bittersweet.

In an attempt to find that opportunity, Wong moved to England. The European cinema didn't have a problem with casting Wong in any role they chose.

She shot films in the UK and in Germany, playing a wide variety of characters. This success was *also* bittersweet.

Wong was an American, born and raised, and she longed to play these satisfying parts back home in the United States. After much success in Europe, Paramount Pictures offered Wong a contract in Los Angeles. They promised she'd be playing lead roles, and Wong jumped at the chance.

Ultimately, she was disappointed. The roles were big, but she was back to playing stereotyped characters. When she did audition for meaty Asian roles, directors rejected her. She was too Chinese to play Chinese in Hollywood. Her career slowly faded, not because she lacked talent or fame. It was all due to the fact that Hollywood wasn't ready for an actress of color to be a leading lady.

Wong faded from the screen, but she never stopped acting. Taking to theater, she found a place to play the characters that excited her. But years of disappointment and quiet activism had worn her down. She stopped seeking out film opportunities— so different from the little girl who used to beg for bit parts.

She passed away at the age of fifty-six, her legacy wiped away by time. We're lucky enough to have rediscovered her and all her fifty films. Her interviews have resurfaced, and in her own words, we can hear Anna May Wong clamoring for an equal chance at her American dream.

Mary & Carrie Dann

Mary & Carrie Dann

1922–2005 ~ 1932–

In 1868, the people of the Western Shoshone tribe signed an agreement with the U.S. government. Called the Treaty of Ruby Valley, this peace accord was a gift from the Western Shoshone.

It granted the government the right to travel safely through their lands, to build a railroad line, and to mine some of the gold found there. Not once did it agree to give up any rights to Western Shoshone land.

Western Shoshone elders Mary and Carrie Dann started their fight in 1972 to force the government to keep the terms of that agreement.

These sisters lived in a house powered by a generator, heated by a woodstove, and made their living raising horses and cattle. Deeply connected to the land where the Western Shoshone had always lived, they let their livestock graze openly.

Over time, the government seized bits and pieces of the property. Eventually, it claimed 80 percent of the Western Shoshones' historical lands. There was gold and silver to be mined, and that was more important than some old **treaty**.

That's not how the Danns saw it. They had an agreement, and they hadn't changed the terms— therefore, they had the right to continue to live and farm where they always had. Their cattle grazed on Western Shoshone land, just as they always had.

Then the Bureau of Land Management started to demand that the Danns and the other Western Shoshone pay grazing fees for their cattle. They arrested Mary Dann for trespassing. What had she done? Taken a walk where she'd always walked, for seventy-four years! Where her parents and grandparents had walked before her!

The Danns refused to accept this. Protesting all the way, they and the Western Shoshone went to court. They wanted the government to abide by their treaty. After all, they had signed it willingly!

In 1979, the U.S. Court of Claims agreed:

the government had illegally taken over Western Shoshone land.

The Danns were thrilled. All they wanted was the government to respect the Treaty of Ruby Valley. Instead, the government awarded them twenty-six million dollars for the use of the land.

This wasn't acceptable. Not to the Danns, and not to the Western Shoshone. Almost everyone in the tribe voted not to accept the money. They weren't interested in selling; they never had been. They just wanted the government to uphold its part of the treaty.

Instead, the Bureau of Land Management sued the Danns for trespassing. They rounded up their cattle and gave them away. Heartbroken, Carrie Dann said, "I was **indigenous** and in one single evening they made me indigent. If you think the Indian wars are over, then think again."

The Dann sisters went on to form the Western Shoshone Defense Project. This project advocates for Western Shoshone rights, as they were laid out in the Treaty of Ruby Valley. It protests the creeping government intrusion on their lands. Because now, guess what? They want to dump nuclear waste there!

Though Mary Dann died in 2005, her sister

carries on through the WSDP. They have congress-people on their side now: agents of the government who agree that the Western Shoshone never gave up their rights to their land.

For now, Carrie Dann remains steadfast. She abides by the Treaty of Ruby Valley. Now she's waiting for the U.S. government to do the same.

FIRSTS!

The world's first known author and poet, Enheduanna recorded her work on clay tablets. More than four thousand years ago, this Sumerian high priestess of Inanna wrote at least three books of hymns—but she also wrote personal poems about the world she lived in, her life, her feelings, and her philosophies on war and suffering.

Ada Lovelace

Ada Lovelace
(Augusta Ada King, Countess of Lovelace)
1815–1852

Debut season was a special time for a young woman in nineteenth-century England.

A series of grand, glittering parties, this flourish of balls signified her official introduction to the world. Most girls hoped to find a husband during their season. Ada Lovelace found something else entirely: the future of computer programming.

At seventeen, Lovelace had already acquired a lifelong love of science and mathematics. Her mother not only encouraged this fascination but insisted on it. She was afraid if Lovelace wasn't directed, she'd fall into creative insanity!

Inquisitive and methodical, Lovelace first showed her scientific bent when she was twelve years old. Deciding that she wanted to fly, she studied flying animals. She created wing diagrams and collected her data into an extensive set of notes. Perhaps silk would make the best wing for a human? Perhaps paper?

Then at seventeen, she met Charles Babbage during her debut. He was in his forties and widowed—theoretically a good marriage catch. Lovelace, however, was more interested in his Difference Engine.

This was an early version of a calculator. To get the answer to complicated math problems, Babbage needed only to turn a crank to make the cogwheels turn inside. The machine did the arithmetic and offered up the answer.

The very next day, Lovelace visited Babbage at home to get a look at this wonderful device. To her disappointment, she discovered that it wasn't yet finished.

Still, the principles behind it fascinated her, and she struck up a friendship with Babbage. They wrote letters to each other from 1835 through 1852.

Midway through their friendship, Babbage decided he wanted to invent an Analytical Engine. This would take his (unfinished) work on the Difference Engine and expand it. He convinced another mathematician to write a paper about the Analytical Engine.

They Did What?

The problem was that paper was in French. Fortunately, Lovelace spoke fluent French. She started the translation right away. As she worked, however, she discovered that neither Babbage nor the paper's writer *truly* understood what an Analytical Engine could do.

Appending the paper with her own notes, Lovelace ended up writing three times as much material about the engine as the original author did.

In it, she pointed out that the engine would be able to do any number of extraordinary things: work higher mathematics, automatically generate music, and more.

All it needed was a program.

And there, in her notes, Ada Lovelace wrote the very first computer program, one that would calculate Bernoulli numbers. These are a series of rational numbers defined by the exponential generating function. An integral part of trigonometry, Bernoulli numbers are used for analysis and number theory. On paper, the equation looks like this:

$$\frac{x}{e^x - 1} = \sum_{n=0}^{\infty} \frac{B_n\, x^n}{n!}$$

That's right. Lovelace banged out a program on a

proto-computer to do that math automatically— just as an *example*!

Even Babbage admitted that Lovelace understood the potential of his Analytical Engine better than he did. He was simply a machinist. She was a visionary.

In the end, the creativity that Lovelace's mother had hoped to squash with numbers allowed her daughter to see clearly the future of computer programming. In her own words, Lovelace explained it like this:

Imagination has two parts. The first one is the ability to make connections between unrelated subjects. The second, she called the Discovering Faculty. She said, "It is that which penetrates into the unseen worlds around us, the worlds of Science."

There's no doubt that Lovelace had that Discovering Faculty. She understood programming in a time when electrical telegraphs were the most cutting edge of technology!

FIRSTS!

Historically, women have graced a lot of currency! In the beginning, the women depicted on coins were usually goddesses. The first coin to feature a real woman was minted in Egypt, around 285 BCE. It featured Queen Berenike I, the second wife of Ptolemy II. The first woman to put her own face on a coin was Persian princess Amastris, around 323 BCE.

The first woman ever to appear on a United States coin was equal rights crusader Susan B. Anthony. She was the face of the dollar coin from 1979 to 1981. She was not the last: Helen Keller appears on the 2003 Alabama state quarter, and the current dollar coin features a portrait of Sacagawea.

The most valuable coin featuring a woman is worth four *million* dollars. This is no ordinary chunk of pocket change. This special coin, created by the

Royal Canadian Mint to celebrate Queen Elizabeth II, weighs 220 pounds (100 kilos,) and it's as big around as a manhole cover! People were so delighted by this novelty that the RCM created several more to sell to collectors.

HARD-CORE BATTLE QUEENS

The Maya boasted a warrior queen who ruled during the fifth century AD. The military governor for the Wak Kingdom, Lady K'abel held the rank of Kaloomte—"supreme warrior"—a rank higher than the king's.

Originally, people thought that Lady K'abel was just a legend. There was no evidence that she had ever been anything more than a story. All that changed when archaeologists discovered her tomb in Guatemala. History and archaeology proved that Lady K'abel existed, ruled, and went to war fifteen hundred years ago in El Perú Waka.

Maria Tallchief

Maria Tallchief
(Elizabeth Marie Tall Chief)
1925–2013

Growing up, everyone called Elizabeth Marie Tall Chief "Betty Marie." That was her name, and she liked it just fine, thanks.

Growing up in a well-to-do family in Osage, Oklahoma, Tallchief enjoyed performing in rodeos, taking piano lessons, and most especially, dancing. She and her sister Marjorie both took ballet.

They excelled at it, and their mother decided to move the family to Los Angeles. Musicals were big business in the 1930s, and Tallchief's mother hoped to find her girls work on the silver screen. At first, Tallchief thought she might become a concert pianist. She loved the music; she felt it in her bones.

That all changed in Los Angeles. There, Tallchief met the dance teacher who changed her life.

Choreographer Bronislava Nijinska was everything a ballet teacher should be: strict, hardworking, and Russian.

In Tallchief, Nijinska found an exciting raw talent to shape. In Nijinska, Tallchief found inspiration. More than anything, she wanted to be a dancer like her teacher. Any lingering dreams she might have had about becoming a concert pianist fell away.

After studying with Nijinska for several years, Tallchief graduated from high school. Originally, she planned to go to college. Her father had other ideas.

He was tired of paying for lessons, he said. It was time for Tallchief to get a job! So she and a friend moved to New York City to look for work.

At the age of seventeen, Tallchief crossed the United States in search of a place for herself as a dancer. When she got to New York City, she found one with a small touring company. It wasn't what she'd planned on, but it was dance, and that's what mattered.

Her old teacher Nijinska turned up in New York, and cast Tallchief as an understudy in her company, Ballet Russe de Monte Carlo. There, Tallchief bloomed into not just a ballerina, but the very first Native American prima ballerina.

With that came new problems, unexpected ones. Company owners encouraged her to change her name, Betty Marie Tallchief, to something more Russian. Maybe Maria Tallchieva, for example. This was a sore spot for Tallchief.

After experiencing discrimination in Los Angeles, she'd already changed her own name a *little*: Tall Chief became Tallchief. That didn't seem like too much of a change. But now they wanted her to erase her heritage completely!

Tallchief refused. The name was hers; she was proud of it. Finally, she compromised on her first name. That's how Betty Marie became Maria, and Maria Tallchief was a star. She dazzled audiences in Paris and New York.

Working with famous choreographer George Balanchine, Tallchief perfected her form. She practiced every single day, even taking extra classes to work on her technique. Growing as a dancer, Tallchief graduated from understudy to lead soloist.

Her performance of the Sugar Plum Fairy in *The Nutcracker* breathed new life into the ballet. Before Tallchief's performance, it hadn't been a very popular show at all. After, it became a regular winter spectacular, all over the United States.

Tallchief performed roles written just for her. She reclaimed roles written for other dancers. Touring the world, she danced in capital cities all over the globe. When televisions cropped up in family rooms, she soon appeared on those screens.

For years, American ballet meant Maria Tallchief. And Maria Tallchief was the name she made and kept for herself—her legacy in her last name, and her destiny in her first. Two worlds combined in a single, fiery dancer.

Oprah Winfrey

Oprah Winfrey
1954—

You know who Oprah Winfrey is. Everybody does.

She's the first (and only) black female billionaire, ever. Building her empire on compassion, empathy, and a talk show watched by millions, Winfrey is so popular that she has her own magazine, lifestyle website, and television network.

When she wants to talk about a book, it becomes an instant bestseller. Once, she even gave away cars to an entire studio audience—because she *could*. Winfrey's influence is so strong that the Texas Cattlemen's Association sued her for saying she was done eating hamburgers. They were afraid *everyone* would stop. Her opinion matters so much that advertisers talk about the "Oprah Effect."

That's an extraordinary amount of power

wielded by a woman whose name isn't even Oprah! Born to a teenage mother in Mississippi, Winfrey's birth certificate lists her as Orpah—a misspelling that Winfrey has chosen to ignore.

As a toddler, Winfrey moved north to live with her grandmother, while her mother tried to make a living as a maid. Mired in poverty, Winfrey didn't enjoy an easy childhood. There was no such thing as a new dress for her. Instead, her grandmother sewed her clothing from old potato sacks.

Though she was smart—Winfrey learned to read by the age of three—her grandmother was strict. If Winfrey misbehaved in any way, her grandmother would beat her with a stick. Still, at her grandmother's house, Winfrey had stability and a sense of order. All that would go away when she turned six, and moved to Milwaukee to live with her mother and her new baby sister.

Unfortunately, before long, Winfrey's mother was having trouble raising both daughters on her salary as a maid. Once again, it was Winfrey who had to move. Sent to live with her father in Nashville, she had no idea that her mother had given birth to another baby girl (and wouldn't find out until she was an adult).

Things turned darker in Nashville. When Winfrey was nine, several family members and a family friend molested her. Separated from her mother, living in a time when people didn't talk about sexual abuse, Winfrey felt trapped. Finally, at the age of thirteen, she ran back to her mother's house in Milwaukee to escape further abuse.

It had taken its toll, though. At only fourteen years old, Winfrey got pregnant. Because she was so young, the pregnancy ended prematurely. The baby boy was born too early and did not survive. This was just one more tragedy in Winfrey's young life.

Soon, she found herself spending time with much older boys, stealing money from her mother's purse and getting in fights at school. Though Winfrey had earned a place at a prestigious honors school nearby, the other students mocked her for her shabby clothes and homemade lunches.

Frustrated, Winfrey's mother sent her back to Nashville to live with her father once more. This time, her father made her education his priority. He was strict, and he insisted that she not just take classes, but that she excel at them. Winfrey blossomed at East Nashville High. An award-winning orator for her school's speech team, she found a job at the local radio station when she was a senior.

When she was seventeen, Winfrey won the Miss Black Tennessee pageant, and continued her education at Tennessee State University. Her engaging personality made her a natural on the local news station, where she got her first adult job. After graduating, she became the first black female news anchor for WLAC-TV in Nashville, and the youngest, too.

From there, Winfrey began her rise to superstardom. Moving to Chicago, she started out with a local talk show, *AM Chicago*. People loved her. The ratings skyrocketed. Soon, Winfrey was beating out legends in the talk-show business like Phil Donohue. Realizing they had a real gem with Winfrey, they renamed the program *The Oprah Winfrey Show*.

The program went on to syndication throughout the entire *world*. It was the most watched talk show ever, and Winfrey won numerous Emmy Awards for it. All through the 1980s and 1990s, Winfrey continued to build her empire. Each year, she hosted a program that she called "My Favorite Things." People clamored for tickets, because they knew Winfrey would be giving those things away. One year, each audience member went home with a brand-new car!

Though she retired her talk show in 2011, Winfrey continues to be a tastemaker. When she talks, people listen. Sometimes she uses her power to recommend really fun holiday gifts. Often, she can't stop talking about a new or classic book she just has to share. However, she always uses her influence to make the world a better place.

Twice, she has advocated for laws to protect kids from child abuse—and those laws passed, with the vocal support of her audience behind them. Having experienced abuse as a child, she wanted to use her power to make sure that other children escaped such horrors.

Because she knows how much her education changed her life, she personally administers scholarships for African American students. Because poverty held her back so often, she funds schools for impoverished and underserved neighborhoods.

It's estimated that Oprah Winfrey has raised more than eighty *million* dollars for worthy causes in her lifetime. Instead of letting her personal tragedies hold her back, she's used them as inspiration. In that process, she literally became the most famous woman in the world.

Iman

Iman
(Iman Mohamed Abdulmajid)
1955–

With an unforgettable face and an imperial presence, Iman is one of the world's most recognizable women.

Born in Mogadishu, Somalia, Iman was a brain before she was a beauty. The daughter of an ambassador and a doctor, she learned to speak five languages fluently.

Iman, which means *faith*, is actually a man's name. Given to her by her mother, the name was a gift, to prepare her for the obstacles she would face in life as a Muslim woman.

Her parents made sure she had an extensive education, sending her to private school, where she flourished. Her life plan led her to study political science, which she pursued at University of Nairobi.

To pay the bills, she worked as a translator.

There, a photographer introduced her to the fashion industry, and the fashion industry fell in love. The first modeling fee Iman asked for was $8,000—the amount she needed to pay her college tuition.

In 1976, she was featured on the cover of *Vogue*—the second black woman ever to do so. Runways and cameras loved her. At nearly six feet tall, and usually one of the few black women on the scene, she stood out as an ethereal beauty.

But remember those brains? Those didn't go away, even as Iman catapulted to fame.

In New York, modeling agencies had different rate cards for women of different races. Iman wasn't having any of that. "I was doing the same job as them," she said. "Why would I get less money?"

Acutely aware of the way she and other women of color were treated in her industry, she wrote two books on the subject. Even though she was a supermodel, Iman had to buy and mix her own cosmetics. The commercial lines available just didn't have makeup suitable for her skin tone.

Rather than wait for the companies to come around, Iman started her own in 1994, catering specifically to women of color.

To this day, Iman continues to talk about the disparity in the way women of color are treated in fashion.

She, along with Bethann Hardison and Naomi Campbell, have asked fashion houses a pointed question: Why do they define beauty as all white? Iman has told them bluntly, "It sends a message that our girls aren't good enough."

Now a businesswoman, a mostly retired supermodel, and an activist, Iman has more than lived up to the challenges her mother worried about when she gave her that name. And now? That name most famously belongs to a spectacular *woman*.

Wilma Mankiller

Wilma Mankiller

1945–2010

The first female Principal Chief of the Cherokee Nation, Wilma Mankiller was shocked when all people wanted to discuss during her campaign was her gender.

That was 1983, and Mankiller figured the Cherokee Nation had much more important matters to consider. **Treaties** signed between the Cherokee Nation and the United States in the nineteenth century were being ignored.

The Cherokee people had been forced to **relocate** to Oklahoma Territory. Promising that this land would belong to them forever, the U.S. government quit upholding its treaties when they discovered gold and oil on Cherokee lands.

Mankiller was born in Tahlequah, Oklahoma, onto one of the few remaining pieces of land that still belonged to her family. Though they were happy in

Oklahoma, they were poor. The Bureau of Indian Affairs promised her father a better life. All he had to do was relocate his family to San Francisco.

Uprooting Mankiller and her ten siblings, the move thrust them into an unfamiliar city. Low-paying jobs were the norm. It was hardly the step up the BIA promised the family.

And for Mankiller, it was a foreign, uncomfortable world. There were streets to play in instead of open land, water came out of taps instead of wells, and nobody spoke Cherokee. At school, people picked on Mankiller—for sounding different, for looking different, and yes, for her unusual last name.

That particularly irritated her, because one of her ancestors had been a soldier. He had guarded the village at night and *earned* the title Mankiller. There was nothing to joke about!

As the civil rights movement swept the United States, Native Americans demanded fair treatment as well. Mankiller said that her life's focus changed on November 20, 1969. On that day, seventy-nine Native Americans seized Alcatraz Island and started what would become a two-year occupation.

It all went back to the treaties—yes, they were

old. But that didn't mean they weren't still valid. Mankiller would later say in a speech at Sweet Briar College, "Just because they're old and because of their age doesn't mean that they're any less valid. The United States Constitution is very old."

Mankiller moved back to her childhood home in Oklahoma. Stepping up, she became a vocal activist for the rights of the Cherokee Nation. This included the right to take care of themselves and their own communities.

Even when outside forces tried to help, they still only came up with plans like relocating **indigenous** families thousands of miles from home.

So that's why Mankiller was surprised that anyone cared that she was a woman when she ran for Deputy Chief. But since they did care, she knew exactly how she would deal with the protests against her. Resolutely, quietly, and firmly.

Mankiller didn't argue when one of the council tried to shout her down. Instead, she had his microphone turned off. It forced him to stop shouting and to start talking with her.

When a college escort insisted that she couldn't be called "Chief" because she was a woman, she ignored the demeaning alternates he suggested. Finally, she told him that Ms. Chief would do just fine.

Serving as Principal Chief for ten years, Mankiller founded the Cherokee Nation Community Development Department. She knew that if the Cherokee people were given the opportunity to build up their own communities, they would. She wasn't disappointed.

Her parents provided Mankiller with books, with opportunity, and with the fervent belief that no one had the right to define her except herself. Mankiller took that to heart, and became a Chief of her nation, *for* her nation.

Josephine Baker

Josephine Baker

1906–1975

When most people hear the name "Josephine Baker," they immediately think of a lithe, winking dancer wearing a skirt made from bananas. Just bananas!

And it's true that Baker became one of the world's most famous **Jazz Age** entertainers. It was in her blood—her father sang and danced in **vaudeville** shows. Her mother aspired to be a music hall dancer.

Baker learned to love the spotlight. She dropped out of school at the age of thirteen. To support herself, she danced on street corners for tips. The St. Louis Chorus vaudeville show caught a glimpse of her and decided to hire her.

She found herself on a fast track to New York, where she starred in the stage productions *Chocolate Dandies* and *Shuffle Along*. Not only was she a fantastic dancer, she had a great sense of humor. Never afraid to make a funny face or to go for a comic moment, Baker delighted audiences.

About this time, France was obsessed with the American Jazz Age. They imported bands, singers—and dancers, like Josephine Baker. She went to Paris in 1925 and stole the show in *La Revue Nègre*. France loved Baker, and Baker loved France.

She decided to move there, to perform there full time. Unlike back in the United States, she didn't have to play in **segregated** clubs. If she wanted to go to a store, she could walk through any door and be welcome. She rocketed to superstardom.

People lined up around the building to get a chance to see her perform. They never knew when she might appear on the stage (or the street!) with her pet cheetah, Chiquita. Baker bought a château for herself and made herself at home.

An American born and raised, Baker did return to the United States. Landing a role in the famed Ziegfeld Follies, Baker hoped she would enjoy the same kind of success at home that she had in France. Ultimately, she was disappointed.

People were hostile toward Baker, the only black

dancer in a sea of white performers. They refused to let her sit in the very nightclubs and restaurants where she performed. *The New York Times* even described her as a Negro wench!

Soon after, Baker returned to her beloved France, back to a life where she was not only famous but equal. She found her peace there. Then when World War II broke out, she found a way to fight for peace, too.

Because she was so popular, Baker could travel into **Axis** countries like Germany and Italy without raising suspicion. After all, she was just a performer—those boxes full of sheet music in her trunk were packed away for her next routine.

Except, secretly, Baker spied for the French Resistance. Her sheet music bore secret messages in invisible ink. Her fame allowed her to visit places that would have otherwise been off-limits. That made it possible for her to smuggle pictures of military installations and copies of plans back to the **Allied** leaders.

During the war, she earned a promotion to sublieutenant in the Women's Auxiliary Air Force. When the war was over, she accepted the prestigious Croix de Guerre (Cross of War, for extraordinary service) as well as the Medal of the Resistance from the French government.

Though she was never as famous at home as she was in France, Baker returned to the United States to fight racism alongside Dr. Martin Luther King Jr. She held boycotts of segregated theaters and clubs, and marched on Washington in protest.

Josephine Baker is remembered best for her Danse Banane (Banana Dance). But she should also be remembered for her service during wartime, and her vigorous support of civil rights.

Her adopted home of France certainly did. When she passed away, she was the first and only American woman to be buried with full French military honors.

Ellen Ochoa

Ellen Ochoa
1958–

When Ellen Ochoa was growing up in La Mesa, California, she didn't plan to become an astronaut.

Why? Because there were no female astronauts at the time. She didn't realize she *could* be one. So Ochoa applied her keen mind to other sciences.

First, she earned a bachelor's degree in physics. After that came her master's of science, and then her doctorate in electrical engineering.

What was she doing with all these advanced degrees? Inventing special optic systems that process digital information. One of them recognizes objects in an image; another can detect the visual noise in an image and remove it.

She did much of this work at NASA. They hired her as a research scientist while she was still in graduate school. Managing the Intelligent Systems Technology Branch for NASA, Ochoa's love of space and space exploration grew.

In 1990, NASA selected her to become an astronaut. Three years later, she earned a place as a mission specialist on the space shuttle *Discovery.*

During that mission, Ochoa and the other scientists aboard conducted tests of the atmosphere and ozone layer. During that mission, she also became the first Latina to go to space!

Since then Ochoa has logged more than a thousand hours in space, spread over four missions. Shortly after her last spaceflight, she was promoted to deputy director of flight crew operations. A pretty good choice—she knew an awful lot about being part of those flight crews.

Ochoa had been to the stars and back, but she wasn't finished rising. In 2012, she earned another promotion. This time, she became the director of Johnson Space Center. Only the second woman ever to hold the position, she is also the first Latina director.

Another achievement? She's quite possibly the first person ever to play the flute in space! According to Ochoa, it's not much different from playing it on earth—except weightlessness held the instrument up for her!

Francesca Caccini

Francesca Caccini

1587–1640

Even among a constellation of musical stars in her family, Francesca Caccini shone the brightest of all.

Educated in Latin and Greek, a gifted instrumentalist and singer, Caccini started her career with the influential Renaissance courts of the Medicis early. In 1600, she dazzled Maria de Medici and Henry IV of France while performing with her family.

King Henry thought "La Cecchina" was the best musician in all of France. He loved her so much, he tried to hire her away from her home of Florence, Italy. The Florentine government absolutely refused to let their songbird go. When she performed her own composition at Carnival, the Florentine Medici court snapped her up to be a court musician. After all, she could play at least six instruments, she sang beautifully, *and* she was a composer! As part of one of the grandest Renaissance courts in the world, Caccini became the highest-paid (and most famous!) musician in Florence.

Now able to devote all her time to music, Caccini wrote the first opera by a woman in 1625. This masterwork was called *La Liberazione di Ruggiero*, which she wrote to celebrate a state visit from Crown Prince Ladislaus Sigismondo. He liked the opera so much that he ordered another performance of it in his native Poland. Plus, he commissioned two more operas from her!

Caccini wrote madrigals and ballads, duets and hymns, and hundreds of solo works. Unfortunately, only a few of them still exist. Most of her elegant compositions are lost to time and history, but the ones that survive still shine a spotlight on her.

Her use of a repeating harmony-melody, called a romanesca, is still studied by contemporary students of music. And there's always an opera company excited to perform *La Liberazion di Ruggerio*.

Despite her own fame as a musician, Caccini refused to let her daughter Margherita perform in a staged comedy. Even though Caccini had performed, and written, any number of staged comedies in her life, she wouldn't let her daughter follow her blazing musical path.

Why?

She was afraid it would ruin Margherita's reputation!

Hedy Lamarr

Hedy Lamarr

1914–2000

She was known as the most beautiful woman in the world, but Hedy Lamarr *should* have been known as one of the smartest.

The star of more than thirty films, Lamarr is remembered for her cascade of black hair, her pale skin, and her ruby-red lips. Everyone agreed she wasn't a very good actor. But she was so nice to look at, the audience clamored for more of her.

Despite that, she didn't take silver-screen stardom all that seriously. Once, she said, "Any girl can be glamorous. All you have to do is stand still and look stupid." As clever as the quip was, it's hard to believe Lamarr could manage to look stupid.

During World War II, she and film composer George Antheil strayed away from the soundstages.

Their contribution to the war effort was technology.

Specifically, it was a method to use different radio frequencies to encode messages. Since the transmission, and not the message, was encoded, Nazi code breakers couldn't spy on the **Allies'** secret military **communiqués.**

They patented their "secret communication system," then donated the patent to the U.S. government. Not only was it very useful during the war, this spread-spectrum technology opened a door to the future.

Without it, we wouldn't have cell phones, WiFi, fax machines . . . the list goes on and on. They actually pioneered the science behind wireless communications, sixty years before we had the foundation in place to use it.

That's right. Lamarr's visionary invention was so far head of its time, the future had to catch up with *her*! Every time you use your tablet or cell phone, each time you connect to a Bluetooth device, think about it.

You may not ever have seen her movies, but you have screen siren Hedy Lamarr to thank for your wireless world!

Diane Humetewa

Diane Humetewa

1964–

A member of the sovereign Hopi Tribe in Arizona, Diane Humetewa grew up steeped in her culture.

Many of her friends were sent away to boarding school. Humetewa, however, started school on the Hualapai Reservation. When she wasn't studying, she explored Arizona's Indian Country with her father. He worked for the Bureau of Indian Affairs, an agency that tries to mediate between Native Americans and the U.S. government.

As she grew up, she learned about the inequalities and injustices often suffered by Native Americans in the United States. Compassionate and whip smart, Humetewa decided the best way to make a difference was to go to law school.

She didn't want to go far away, though. She wanted

to be able to work for her community, and that meant sticking with Arizona State University for college.

Graduating from their Sandra Day O'Connor College of Law, Humetewa started her career in private practice. She represented tribal governments in court and became an expert in Indian law.

Later, serving as the first Native American woman appointed to the U.S. Attorney's Office, she specialized in prosecuting cultural crimes, violent crimes in Indian Country, and archaeological crimes. She worked hard to build a relationship between the U.S. government and Arizona's Native people.

Considered the foremost expert on Native American law, Humetewa is also a passionate defender of victims' rights. She's dedicated much of her work to helping the people most affected by crimes. In fact, she founded one of the first federal victim services programs in the United States.

Humetewa has served as a judge for the Hopi Tribe since 2002. In 2014, she was nominated to be first female Native American federal judge. (She's also the third Native American federal judge *ever*, and the only one currently active!)

Not often unanimous, the Senate voted 96–0 to confirm her.

Julia Child

Julia Child

1912–2004

Julia Child is remembered for dropping a turkey during a television cooking demonstration.

Except, it was really a potato cake, and you know what? She never even planned to become a chef, let alone an internationally celebrated one! To think she would earn her fame by introducing French cuisine to home cooks, to her, was ridiculous.

At six feet two inches, Child thought that she would distinguish herself in college basketball. Unfortunately for her, the school changed the rules. She had only a jump game and—yep!—the school banned the jump game. So much for basketball.

The start of World War II inspired Child to join the military. This time, she planned to join the Women's Army Corps (WACs) or the U.S. Navy's

Women Accepted for Volunteer Emergency Service (WAVES). Once more, circumstances derailed her plans. She was much too tall to serve in those organizations.

Disappointed, Child joined the Office of Strategic Services as a typist. Eventually, she became a research assistant in the Secret Intelligence division. That's right, before she was a cook, Julia Child was a spy!

It wasn't until she had a special dinner in Rouen, France, that she realized she wanted to learn to cook. This time, nobody would stop her!

By all accounts, she was a pretty terrible chef in the beginning. Her kitchen experiments were usually kitchen disasters. She failed again and again.

But Child was determined to press on. She *really* wanted to learn the art of French cuisine. So she attended the famous Le Cordon Bleu cooking school in France. Then she took private lessons from more accomplished chefs in the field. Joining a cooking club, she made friends with two other passionate cooks, Louisette Bertholle and Simone Beck.

Together, the three of them decided to write a complete guide to French cooking. Child translated it into English, and when finished, the cookbook was humongous. Some publishers said it was way too long to publish—but Child still wouldn't give up.

Eventually, one publisher took a chance on *Mastering the Art of French Cooking*. It was a smash hit. The book was a huge bestseller in the United States, and Child became a star. People loved her; she helped home cooks realize that they could create edible masterpieces, too.

Child's cheerful personality and her passion to share French cuisine led to television presentations. Those turned into television series, which eventually led to the infamous turkey, er, potato cake episode.

She tried to turn her potato cake over by flipping it into the air and back into the pan. Instead, it fell onto the stove, breaking into pieces. Child had tons of experience when it came to the unexpected. She'd learned a lot from her many attempts to become a great chef.

She put the cake back in her pan and told the audience, "You see, when I flipped it, I didn't have the courage to do it the way I should have."

That summed up Child's career perfectly. If she hadn't had the courage to fail at cooking, she never would have become a great chef. The proof was in the potato cake!

Harriet Tubman

Harriet Tubman
(Araminta Ross)
c. 1822–1913

Born into slavery, escaped into freedom, Araminta Ross changed her name to Harriet Tubman and became something better than a legend. She became an icon. What's surprising is that most of us know only part of the story.

Harriet Tubman is best known as a conductor on the Underground Railroad. Leading enslaved people to freedom in New York and Canada, she guided them with a firm sense of purpose.

She had confidence in her mission, but she also carried a pistol with her. If someone changed their mind, everyone's safety would be in danger. The pistol helped Tubman not so gently warn people that there would be no turning back.

Later, Tubman said, "I was the conductor of the

Underground Railroad for eight years, and I can say what most conductors can't say: I never ran my train off the track, and I never lost a passenger."

If this were all Tubman had accomplished in her life, she would still be an extraordinary woman. But after thirteen years on the Railroad and conducting at least seventy enslaved people to freedom, she went to war. Literally.

During the Civil War, she ran spy missions into Confederate territory. Though it was dangerous, Tubman always made it back safely—with invaluable information. It was her intelligence gathering and tactics that led to the raid on the Combahee Ferry in South Carolina.

The first woman to command American troops in war, Tubman and a platoon of African American soldiers stormed the plantations around the Combahee River. They burned houses, outbuildings, commissaries, and cotton warehouses. Commanding the water, they destroyed the ferry and the bridge.

When the local enslaved people realized that Union gunships were on the river, they liberated themselves. Carrying children and livestock, bags of grain and their meager possessions, nearly *eight hundred* people escaped slavery during the raid. Afterward, Tubman gave a rousing speech to celebrate their victory.

After the war ended, Tubman didn't rest. She traveled, giving speeches about equality and liberty. Raising awareness of injustice and conquering it whenever she could is how Tubman spent much of her time.

She worked alongside Susan B. Anthony, fighting for women's voting rights. In her later years, she donated some of her land to open a home for poor, elderly African Americans.

Once, Harriet Tubman swore, "I would fight for my liberty so long as my strength lasted," and she did. Most people know her best for her time on the Underground Railroad.

But now you know that she spent a lifetime crusading for equal rights—for *everyone.*

MAD, BAD, AND DANGEROUS TO KNOW

If your only experience with leaders of Madagascar is King Julien, let me introduce you to a real one who makes him look positively reasonable.

Ranavalona I of Madagascar was exactly not thrilled when her husband died. The heir to the throne (not her, and not her children, because she didn't have any) wanted to let the British Empire take over in exchange for weapons. Uh, no.

Ranavalona staged a coup—which means she basically raised a small army and took over the country by force. The only reason the royal guards knew there was a new empress in town was because they found her on the throne.

So far, sounds pretty normal, right? Well . . . except for the guys she had stabbed in the stomach thirty times for opposing her rise to power. Then there was the guard whom she summoned, and then executed for abandoning his post.

The thing is, Ranavalona kept Madagascar free of colonialist invasion, which was awesome. On the other hand, she made it illegal to dance, sing, bathe, sleep on a mattress, clap hands, or look in a mirror for a year after her husband's death. Punishment? Being sold into slavery.

Of course, enslaving people worked out pretty well for Ranavalona. She happened to enslave one Frenchman who singlehandedly **industrialized** her nation. Ranavalona held off invaders, would-be assassins, and colonial infiltrators until her death at eighty-three.

Frida Kahlo

Frida Kahlo

1907–1954

One of the most celebrated artists in Mexican history, Frida Kahlo wasn't supposed to become a painter.

Born in a blue house that stands to this day, Kahlo was a vibrant, active child. She ran the streets, she boxed—she was rarely still. When the Mexican Revolution broke out, she continued to play outside. Any time gunfire broke out, Kahlo's mother forced her inside the little blue house to safety.

A revolution couldn't slow Kahlo down, but polio did. She got sick when she was six. The virus withered the muscles in one of her legs. Her hips and spine grew distorted, making it painful to walk. Still, that didn't keep her from working toward her goals.

She was one of thirty-five girls invited to study at Escuela Nacional Preparatoria, one of Mexico's elite schools. History, language, and culture fascinated her. Especially attracted to the history of Mexico and its people, Kahlo dressed in native shirts and skirts, embellished with scarves and flowers in her hair.

An inquisitive student, Kahlo was on track to become a physician. Then tragedy changed her fate. The bus she was riding crashed into a trolley. The impact broke Kahlo's spine, collarbone, ribs, pelvis, and legs. The next three months were torture, spent in a full body cast.

It took Kahlo more than a year to recover. Before the accident, Kahlo had enjoyed boxing and other sports. Though she had been disabled by the polio, she was still active. After the accident, she was confined to her bed so she started painting. Her mother made her an easel; she got her paints and supplies from her father. Isolated in her recovery, Kahlo painted her pain, her emotions, her face. Unlike other artists, Kahlo said, "I never painted dreams. I painted my own reality."

And art was her new reality. She showed her work to a famous muralist, Diego Rivera. Not only did he encourage her to keep painting, he became a mentor to her. However, she always remained a muse to herself. Her rich colors and surrealist style dazzled art lovers around the world.

After her accident, Kahlo never spent another day without pain. But she spent all of those days with her paintings. She said she herself was the subject she knew best. Among her works are paintings of her undergoing surgery, portraits with monkeys, her broken body, and her bold eyebrows and facial hair. People hailed her work—a mix of surrealism, self-portrait, and **indigenous** Mexican techniques—as visionary.

Kahlo didn't have a long career. Always ill and injured, she died at the age of forty-seven. Her work is her legacy, and it's a grand one. Her paintings have sold for more than any other female artist aside from Mary Cassatt.

Now, her little blue house is a museum: the Museum of Frida Kahlo. Full of her art, artifacts, and her strikingly familiar clothing, it's a monument to a young woman who planned to be a doctor but instead became a legend.

Alice Walker

Alice Walker
1949–

The first African American woman to win the Pulitzer Prize for literature, Alice Walker has spent her career amplifying unheard voices.

The child of sharecroppers in Georgia, Walker had very little except family and stories while she was growing up. The 1940s were tough for everyone. It was wartime; food was rationed, and everyone had to work twice as hard to get by.

Walker's mother emphasized the importance of reading and writing, in defiance of a community that believed black people didn't need an education. Ridiculous! When she was just four years old, Walker entered the first grade. She *would* get an education!

When she was only seven years old, Walker's life changed in an instant. One of her brothers shot her in the eye with a BB gun. He did it on purpose, but she kept that to herself. Afraid of her parents' reaction, she claimed it was an accident.

Without a car, Walker had to wait a whole week to get to the doctor. That delay cost her the sight in her right eye. A white scar formed, a visible reminder of her injury.

Self-conscious, Walker retreated from the schoolmates who taunted her. Turning to writing, she spilled out her thoughts and feelings on paper—but she kept them a secret. Already vulnerable, she didn't want anyone to know about the lyrical, personal places she went to inside her own mind.

In high school, Walker had surgery to remove the scar. Older and more confident, she rose to the top of her class. Voted class queen, and earning her place as the valedictorian, Walker discovered something important.

Life before the scar had taught her to look at people for who they really were. Because of that, in her life after, she had the patience to wait and see how people turned out.

From high school, Walker went to Spelman College. She earned a full scholarship there, then eventually transferred to Sarah Lawrence College to finish her degree. Walker wrote essays and poetry; she was an activist in the civil rights movement and spoke out about women's rights as well.

One of her early essays for *Ms.* magazine reintroduced the world to African American author Zora Neale Hurston. It was important to Walker to amplify black voices. So often, they were drowned out and ignored—Walker wanted to change that.

Walker wrote steadily even as she worked tirelessly. In the 1970s, she published two novels. She based one on her social work experiences—this was a way to be creative and an activist at the same time.

Then in 1982, Alice Walker published the novel that changed her life forever. It was called *The Color Purple*, and it was about a woman named Celie, who struggled to break free from abuse in her family, and fought against the racism of the world outside her home.

Heartbreaking and illuminating, *The Color Purple* was a bestseller and a critical hit. The following year, Walker won the National Book Award for it—and became the first African American woman to win the Pulitzer Prize in literature.

The book moved so many people that Hollywood adapted it into an Academy Award–winning film, and Broadway produced a musical based on it. Suddenly, the world knew who Alice Walker was, and they wanted to hear more.

Walker continued to write. She continued to fight for equal rights, for people everywhere. Four decades out of college, Walker never slows down. Publishing volumes of poetry, memoirs, and novels, Walker tirelessly amplified her message to the world.

For a young woman who used to keep her writings secret, Alice Walker is now the woman who uses her writing to change the world!

HARD-CORE BATTLE QUEENS

In the fifth century BC, Artemisia I of Caria ruled Ionia proudly and strategized with Xerxes, the leader of the Persians. A brilliant tactical mind, Artemisia warned Xerxes that the Greeks would best them in a battle at sea. Xerxes ignored her, so Artemisia joined the Battle of Salamis as the commander of five ships.

During the fight, she successfully camouflaged her **trireme** as one of the enemy ships. Slipping among them, unnoticed, Artemisia wreaked havoc among the unsuspecting Greeks and turned the battle in her favor.

Which Fabulous
Lady of History Are You?

Curious about your historical soul twin? Take this quick quiz and match yourself with a famous bestie!

1. You have a really big test coming up. It's not your favorite subject, and your best friend just invited you to the movies. You . . .

A) Review your notes quickly, then head to the movies. Your serious side won't let you blow off homework, but your fun-loving side won't let you blow off a night out with your friends!

B) Have already studied every single detail you need to know about this test. What you don't know is who's going to be sitting next to each other at the movies and you really need to find out.

C) Forget that test. You'll conquer it later. Right now, it's time for Junior Mints at the concession stand.

D) Take a rain check on the movie. Doing well on this test is important, and you want to set a good example for your little sister.

E) Study a little. Then movies. Then study more. Then maybe stop at a comic-book store.

2. It's Spring Break, woo-hoo! Two responsibility-free weeks—you're going to enjoy them by . . .

A) Dressing up in wacky costumes and learning the steps to the hottest new dances. You might even invent some!

B) Reading everything your friends post online. You don't want to miss the latest gossip.

C) Gathering your army (okay, your siblings) and storming the beach without mercy!

D) Protesting the destruction of your town's two-hundred-year-old oak tree. Who needs another cell phone tower? That tree is an important part of your history!

E) Figuring out what would happen if Future You could send texts to Current You. That could be awesome. Or terrible. Is that your phone chirping? Hurry, it might be Future You!

3. More than anything, you want people to remember you as . . .

A) A star, baby.

B) You don't need to be remembered. You've written it all down so people get the story right!

C) Fierce.

D) A good leader.

E) Hilarious. Or spacy. Or spacylarious. Spaylarious? Hilacy?

4. There's someone new in your class at school. She looks kind of lost and lonely. What do you do?

A) Make a face at her to make her laugh. A good laugh makes everybody feel better.

B) You're pretty shy and quiet yourself, so you let her find her own way. If she catches your eye, you'll give her an encouraging nod.

C) Give her one chance to do everything you say. Or else.

D) Step up! You understand that when someone is lost and afraid, a leader can help her find their way.

E) Forget that she's a stranger and make a place for her at your lunch table with all your friends. You guys will be best buds in no time!

5. The three words that best describe you are . . .

A) Exciting, energetic, and vibrant.

B) Eloquent, observant, and literary.

C) Strong, tenacious, and imposing.

D) Powerful, determined, and confident.

E) Funny, and nice, but nice sounds an insult, even though you don't mean it that way; it's kind of like neat. You think things are really genuinely neat, but sometimes people think you're being sarcastic, and you're not. Neat is just . . . neat!

6. Of all the pets in all the world, you would love to have . . .

A) A cheetah named Chiquita.

B) An African Grey parrot—they can repeat whole conversations.

C) A couple hundred doves.

D) Maybe not a pet, but you'd love to help save endangered species from extinction.

E) Dog. Cat. Fish. Hamster. Guinea pig. Bird. Rock. Anything small or portable!

7. A friend borrows your favorite book, then loses it. She's pretending like it didn't happen. You . . .

A) Keep asking for it, because if you can convince her that the book is really important, she will change her mind about keeping it.

B) Write a witty story about a certain book hoarder, cleverly disguising everyone's identity.

C) Tell her it's okay, you're not mad. Then blackmail her later.

D) Realize the best way to get your book back is to rally against her by gaining followers.

E) Tell her jokes until she's laughing, then nicely ask for it back. Laughter makes everything easier!

8. You're taking a personality quiz, and you recognize a pattern in the answers. You . . .

A) Pick randomly. Better yet, close your eyes and point. Who knows what you might turn into!

B) Consider which answer would reflect best on you and your goals, then choose them deliberately.

C) Don't care. The only answer is your answer, and you will choose your answer faithfully.

D) Realize that you can control the outcome of the quiz. You're the one in charge of your destiny. (But you do look at the answers to see if you were correct.)

E) Have taken this quiz before. You must have. Because you're not psychic, so you couldn't have seen these answers in a dream. (Or maybe you did. Did you? Are you psychic? Quick, try to predict the lottery numbers.)

Count up your answers. If you have 5 of any single letter, that's your history twin! If you have 4/4, then you're a split decision. If you have a little bit here or there, then you're every fabulous woman in every fabulous way and 100 percent uniquely you!

MOSTLY A: Isn't this just the kittens mittens? You're Josephine Baker! (p.209) You love clowning around, and you're not afraid of taking center stage, ever. You might not be appreciated in your own time, but one day everyone will realize you were always a star.

MOSTLY B: We don't know your real name, but quizzically speaking, you're Murasaki Shikibu. (p.127) With your eyes and ears open, you pay attention to everyone's details. This means you're not only a great writer, you're a great witness to history!

MOSTLY C: Well, well, well. Take no prisoners, huh? Your soul twin is Olga of Kiev. (p.161) Sure, the Russians made *her* a saint, but you're more likely to end up sitting alone at lunch if you're not careful!

MOSTLY D: You're Anna Maria Chávez (p.85)—smart, ambitious, and deeply passionate about environment and historical legacy. You could run the world one day—or the Girl Scouts! (Or both!)

MOSTLY E: Ooh, you're comedian Ellen DeGeneres! (p.95) Your upbeat personality and genuine kindness will get you far in this world. Just keep swimming!

SPLIT DECISION: Minnie Spotted Wolf (p.29) is your history sis! You're constantly surprising people with the things you want to do—but no one is surprised when you achieve them!

Vocabulary Guide

abolitionist—Someone who fought to end slavery and racial inequality through political and social pressure. (Elizabeth Cady Stanton was a suffragette and an abolitionist.)

acumen—The ability to make good, quick decisions, usually in a particular field. (Anna Maria Chávez has a lot of business acumen.)

the Allies—The coalition of United Kingdom, France, and the United States of America during World War II. (Part of the Marine Women's Reserve, Minnie Spotted Wolf operated heavy equipment for the Allies during World War II.)

to assassinate—To kill a political or social leader, usually as a form of protest. (Benazir Bhutto, the former prime minister of Pakistan, was assassinated at a political rally in 2007.)

the Axis—The coalition of Germany, Italy, and Japan during World War II. (Josephine Baker spied on the Axis during the war. No one expected secret messages in her music!)

to beatify—To make a saint. (Margery Kempe wanted the church to beatify her, so she hired a scribe to write her life story.)

Bollywood—Part of the major film industry in India, centered in Mumbai. This word can also describe the kind of movies made in Bollywood—often with elaborate music and dance numbers. (If your Hindi is a little rusty, you can catch Aishwarya Rai Bachchan in the Bollywood-inspired *Bride and Prejudice*.)

communiqué—A very important statement, often released to the press, or by the government. (Eleanor Roosevelt often reviewed the president's communiqués when he was ill.)

concubine—A romantic partner to a king or emperor, lower in status than a wife and usually enslaved. (The Dowager Empress Cixi of China started life as a concubine, but ended it as the nation's sole ruler.)

diplomacy—Carefully managing the opinions and feelings between two different parties, to help come to an agreement or to settle a disagreement. (One of the ways Elizabeth I practiced diplomacy was by offering her hand in marriage to various foreign leaders. As she never had any intention of marrying any of them, she must have been pretty slick!)

dissent—When a judge writes a public disagreement with the majority opinion in a case. (The first female Supreme Court justice, Sandra Day O'Connor, wrote a blistering dissent for *Kelo v. New London*.)

dogfight—An aerial battle that takes place between two or more planes. (Bessie Coleman would be happy to tell you that one tactic you can use to win a dogfight is a whifferdill turn.)

to emancipate—To free someone, usually from a legal or political state. (Teen athlete Salma Kakar rallies to emancipate women in Afghanistan with an unusual kind of protest: she insists on riding her bike.)

expatriate—Someone who leaves his native country to live in another. Often refers to Americans in the early twentieth century who moved to France and Italy as part of an artistic movement. (Find out more about one of the most famous expatriates ever on p. 209—Josephine Baker!)

to immure—To enclose someone in the walls of a building. (In the middle ages, Julian of Norwich immured herself inside a church's walls. She lived out the rest of her life there as an anchoress.)

impediment—An obstacle, error, or injury that makes it hard to accomplish something. (Amelia Bloomer invented new undies after bikes were invented, because petticoats were an impediment to a safe ride.)

indigenous—People native to a region. (The indigenous people of Australia are sometimes referred to as Aborigines, even though they call themselves Maori.)

industrialization—When a society shifts from a primarily agricultural culture to a culture centered around machines and technology. (Industrialization helped

Madam C. J. Walker become the first female self-made millionaire in the United States!)

Jazz Age—The period of time from 1919 to 1929, during the rise of jazz music; one of the first modern fad periods defined by popular culture. (If you want to time travel to the Jazz Age, just listen to Bessie Smith's "Cemetery Blues.")

licentiateship—A license granted, usually by a European university, entitling its bearer to practice certain careers. Ranked above a bachelor's degree but below a master's. (Marie Curie had to go to France to earn her licentiateship in physics.)

lynching—A public execution by a mob; most often used to refer to the hangings and burnings of African Americans in the United States by large groups of white Americans during the 19th and 20th Centuries. (Lynchings claimed more than three thousand lives in the United States between 1882 and 1930.)

Quakerism—A Christian denomination that states all believers are part of the priesthood; it preaches nonviolence, abolition, and sobriety. (Mary Barrett Dyer went to Massachusetts in 1659 to spread the word about Quakerism. She and two other evangelist friends were executed for it.)

regent—Someone who rules on a monarch's behalf, when the monarch is unable to fulfill his or her duties. (Galla Placidia governed as Valentinian III's regent until he came of age.)

regime—A carefully planned system or government, usually referring to an authoritarian shift in power. (The people of the Philippines topped the Marcos regime when they voted for Corazon Aquino to become their new president.)

to relocate—To move a person or a group of people to a new location to live. (The Bureau of Indian Affairs relocated Wilma Mankiller's family from Tahlequah, Oklahoma, to San Francisco, California.)

repast—A meal. (After a life-changing repast in France, Julia Child decided she wouldn't stop until she became a master chef!)

rondeau—A French form of poetry with a repeating phrase that links each stanza to the next. (In medieval France, Christine de Pisan set her romantic rondeaux to music.)

satire—Exaggerating or mocking the shortcomings of others, especially in the form of political speech. (Comedian Wanda Sykes uses satire to bring attention to inequality against women and women of color.)

scathing—Really, really, really, really, seriously incredibly mean. (Known for her scathing wit, Dorothy Parker once said, "Their pooled emotions wouldn't fill a teaspoon.")

to segregate—To separate, generally by racial distinction; usually referring to social mores of the United States after the American Civil War. (When a train conductor tried to force Ida B. Wells into a segregated car, she sued the company—and won!)

stele—A stone or wood monument, usually taller than it is wide. Often sculpted, but sometimes painted. (After a thousand years, we know the name of Maya princess Lady Ikoom because archaeologists found a stele erected in her honor.)

suffrage—Having the right to vote in a democratic election; often used to describe women's suffrage—the movement to grant women the right to vote. (Fusae Ichikawa helped establish the New Woman Association, advocating for women's suffrage in Japan.)

treaty—An agreement between two political entities, usually national governments. (Queen Lili'uokalani of Hawai'i protested the Treaty of Annexation in 1879, but the United States claimed the islands anyway.)

trireme—An ancient Greek ship propelled by three sets of oars. (It took 170 oarsmen and one flute player to drive a trireme. The flautist kept everyone paddling in time with music!)

vaudeville—A popular form of entertainment in the late nineteenth and early twentieth century in North America, mainly comprised of a variety of acts: singing, dancing, comedy, skits, etcetera. (Barbra Streisand earned an Academy Award portraying vaudeville comedienne and singer Fanny Brice.)

Bibliography

Abbey, Susannah. "Chief Wilma Mankiller." *The My Hero Project.* Jeanne Meyers, Karen Pritzker and Rita Milch, n.d. Web. 19 Nov. 2014.

"About." *Official Website of Singer and Actress Audra McDonald.* Audra McDonald, n.d. Web. 21 Nov. 2014.

"Ada Lovelace." *The Babbage Engine.* Computer History Museum, n.d. Web. 13 Nov. 2014.

Addy, E. A. *Ghana History for Primary Schools.* London: Longmans, Green, 1958. Print.

"Aishwarya Rai Bachchan's Old Ads and Modelling Days Pictures." *FilmiBeat.* One India, 27 Sept. 2012. Web. 28 Nov. 2014.

Alice Walker: Beauty in Truth. Dir. Pratibha Parmar. Perf. Alice Walker, Angela Davis, Oprah Winfrey, Jewelle Gomez, Yoko Ono, Sapphire, Gloria Steinem, et al. Kali Films, 2013. DVD.

Appiah, Anthony, and Henry Louis Gates. *Africana: The Encyclopedia of the African and African American Experience: The Concise Desk Reference.* Philadelphia: Running, 2003. Print.

Appleton, Kirsten. "Supreme Court Justice Ruth Bader Ginsburg Embraces 'Notorious R.B.G.' Tees." *ABC News.* ABC News Network, 20 Oct. 2014. Web. 10 Nov. 2014.

"Astronaut Bio: Ellen Ochoa (3/2014)." *Lyndon B. Johnson Space Center.* NASA, n.d. Web. 19 Nov. 2014.

"Audra McDonald Profile." *Broadway.com.* Key Brand Entertainment, n.d. Web. 21 Nov. 2014.

"¡Azúcar! The Life and Music of Celia Cruz." *National Museum of American History.* Smithsonian Institute, n.d. Web. 02 Nov. 2014.

Baker, Lee. "Ida B. Wells-Barnett (1862–1931) and Her Passion for Justice." *People at Duke University.* Duke University, n.d. Web. 28 Nov. 2014.

"Ban Bossy. Encourage Girls to Lead." *Ban Bossy. Encourage*

Girls to Lead. Lean In/Girl Scouts of America, 2014. Web. 28 Nov. 2014.

Bard, Mitchell G. "Estée Lauder." *The Jewish Virtual Library.* The Jewish Virtual Library, 01 Jan. 1998. Web. 15 Nov. 2014.

Beaton, Kate. *Hark!: A Vagrant.* Montréal: Drawn & Quarterly, 2011. Print.

"Billie Jean King." *WTT.com.* Mylan World Team Tennis, n.d. Web. 11 Nov. 2014.

Blay, Zandile. "Iman, Inc." *Scene* 01 Mar. 2014: 46–52. Print.

Cadwalladr, Carole. "Iman: "I Am the Face of a Refugee." *The Guardian.* Guardian News and Media, 28 June 2014. Web. 11 Nov. 2014.

Capriccioso, Rob. "Diane Humetewa, Confirmed to Federal Bench, Makes History." *Indian Country Today.* Indian Country Today Media Network, n.d. Web. 11 Nov. 2014.

Carter, Bill. "At Lunch With: Ellen DeGeneres." *The New York Times.* The New York Times, 12 Apr. 1994. Print.

"Celia Cruz—The Queen of Salsa." *Celia Cruz.* N.p., n.d. Web. 02 Nov. 2014.

Chin-Lee, Cynthia, Megan Halsey, and Sean Addy. *Amelia to Zora: Twenty-Six Women Who Changed the World.* Watertown, MA: Charlesbridge, 2005. Print.

Chisholm '72: Unbought & Unbossed. Dir. Shola Lynch. Perf. Shirley Chisholm, Octavia Butler, Bobby Seale. A REALside Production, 2005. DVD.

"Christine de Pisan." *Encyclopædia Britannica Online.* Encyclopædia Britannica, 2014. Web. 24 Nov. 2014.

"Christine De Pizan." *The Educational Legacy of Medieval and Renaissance Traditions.* Cal Poly Pomona Department of Medieval Studies, n.d. Web. 24 Nov. 2014.

Chua-Eoan, Howard. "The Silent Song of Maria Tallchief." *Time.* 12 Apr. 2013. Web. 29 Nov. 2014.

"The Complete Aishwarya Rai Profile." *Lights, Camera, Bollywood.* Lights, Camera, Bollywood, n.d. Web. 28 Nov. 2014.

Cooney, Kara. *The Woman Who Would Be King.* New York: Crown Group, 2014. Print.

Craft, Kimberly L. *Infamous Lady: The True Story of Countess Erzsébet Báthory.* Lexington, KY: Kimberly L. Craft, 2009. Print.

Dalton, Rex. "An Archaeologist Digs through Her Life." *Nature.com.* Nature Publishing Group, 07 July 2010. Web. 08 Nov. 2014.

Dash, Mike. "The Demonization of Empress Wu." *Smithsonian.* Smithsonian Institute, 10 Aug. 2012. Web. 01 Dec. 2014.

Da Sousa, Vatsala. "Giving an Eye for an Eye." *The Times of India.* Times Group, 29 Aug. 2001. Web. 28 Nov. 2014.

Diamond, Robert. "An Interview with Lea Salonga." *BroadwayWorld.com.* Wisdom Digital Media, 30 Oct. 2005. Web. 28 Nov. 2014.

"Diane J. Humetewa, Professor of Practice." *Sandra Day O'Connor College of Law.* Arizona State University, n.d. Web. 11 Nov. 2014.

"Discovery of Stone Monument at El Perú-Waka' Adds New Chapter to Ancient Maya History." *Newsroom.* Washington University in St. Louis, 16 July 2013. Web. 28 Nov. 2014.

Dowd, Maureen. "What Tina Wants." *Vanity Fair.* Condé Nast, 01 Jan. 2009. Print.

"Dr. Susan La Flesche Picotte." *Changing the Face of Medicine.* U.S. National Library of Medicine, n.d. Web. 22 Nov. 2014.

Dunbar, Brian. "Johnson Space Center Director Dr. Ellen Ochoa." *NASA.* NASA, 01 Jan. 2013. Web. 22 Nov. 2014.

———. "NASA's First Female Hispanic Astronaut Shares Experiences." *NASA.* NASA, 26 June 2003. Web. 22 Nov. 2014.

The Editors of Encyclopædia Britannica. "Julia Child (American Cook and Author)." *Encyclopedia Britannica Online.* Encyclopedia Britannica, 28 June 2013. Web. 22 Oct. 2014.

"Edmonia Lewis." *Encyclopædia Britannica Online.* Encyclopædia Britannica, 2014. Web. 16 Nov. 2014.

"Edmonia Lewis." *The Smithsonian American Art Museum.* Smithsonian Institute, n.d. Web. 16 Nov. 2014.

"Elizabeth Marie Tall Chief." *Bio.* A&E Television Networks, 2014. Web. 29 Nov. 2014.

Essinger, James. *A Female Genius: How Ada Lovelace Started the Computer Age.* New York: Gibson Square, 2013. Print.

"Etta James." *Bio.* A&E Television Networks, 2014. Web. 12 Nov. 2014.

"Etta James: A Life in Music." *The Telegraph.* Telegraph Media Group, 18 Jan. 2002. Web. 12 Nov. 2014.

Farrell, Nancy. "Bessie Coleman." *American Experience: Fly Girls.* PBS, n.d. Web. 02 Nov. 2014.

"First USMC Native American Minnie Spotted Wolf." *Armed Forces History Museum.* Armed Forces Military Museum, n.d. Web. 29 Nov. 2014.

Fitzpatrick, Tommye. "Vera Wang Says Keep Your Feet on the Ground and Don't Get Ahead of Yourself." *Business of Fashion.* Business of Fashion, 30 Apr. 2013. Web. 30 Nov. 2014.

"5 Things You Didn't Know About Josephine Baker." *Mental Floss.* Michael Wolff, n.d. Web. 19 Nov. 2014.

Foley, Bridget. "Ellen DeGeneres." *W Magazine.* Condé Nast, 01 Mar. 2007. Print.

Gates, Henry L., Jr. "Who Was the First Black Millionairess?" *The Root.* The Slate Group, n.d. Web. 30 Nov. 2014.

Giddings, Paula. *Ida: A Sword among Lions: Ida B. Wells and the Campaign against Lynching.* New York: Amistad, 2008. Print.

Gilmore, Glenda E. "She Would Not Be Silent." *Washington Post.* 13 Apr. 2008. Web. 30 Nov. 2014.

Ginsburg, Ruth B., Dorit Beinisch, and Nina Totenberg. "Supreme Court Justice Ruth Bader Ginsburg and Former President of the Supreme Court of Israel Dorit Beinisch in Conversation with Nina Totenberg by 92nd Street Y." *The New Livestream.* The 92nd Street Y, n.d. Web. 10 Nov. 2014.

Graham, Mhairi. "Joan Baez: Musician, Activist and Inspiration." *AnOther.* Another Publishing, n.d. Web. 23 Nov. 2014.

Harness, Cheryl. *Remember the Ladies: 100 Great American Women*. New York: HarperCollins, 2001. Print.

Hassett, Brenna. "Halet Çambel." *TrowelBlazers*. TrowelBlazers, n.d. Web. 08 Nov. 2014.

"Hedy Lamarr: Invention of Spread Spectrum Technology." *Famous Women Inventors*. Invent Help, n.d. Web. 14 Nov. 2014.

Heinemann, Sue. *The New York Public Library Amazing Women in American History: A Book of Answers for Kids*. New York: J. Wiley, 1998. Print.

Henderson, Harry, and Albert Henderson. *The Indomitable Spirit of Edmonia Lewis. A Narrative Biography*. N.p.: n.p., 2012. Print.

Hertz, Stephanie. "Bio." *Destination Iman*. Iman, n.d. Web. 11 Nov. 2014.

Homans, Jennifer. "Maria Tallchief." *The Lives They Lived*. The New York Times Magazine, n.d. Web. 29 Nov. 2014.

Hong, Yunah, Kevin Norton, Eric Lind, Liam Dalzell, and Doan Ly. *Anna May Wong: In Her Own Words*. New York: Women Make Movies, 2011. Film.

Hopwood, Jon C. "Biography." *IMDb. IMDb.com*, n.d. Web. 01 Dec. 2014.

"Human Rights Defenders Carrie Dann and Mary Dann." *Frontline Defenders*. Frontline Defenders, n.d. Web. 09 Nov. 2014.

"Iman Mohamed Abdulmajid." *Bio*. A&E Television Networks, 2014. Web. 11 Nov. 2014.

Jacobs, Laura. *"Our Lady of the Kitchen." Vanity Fair*. Condé Nast, 2009. Print.

James, Etta, and David Ritz. *Rage to Survive: The Etta James Story*. Cambridge, MA: Da Capo, 2003. Print.

Johnson, Ann Donegan, and Steve Pileggi. *The Value of Learning: The Story of Marie Curie*. La Jolla, CA: Value Communications, 1978. Print.

Johnson, Peter. "Minnie Spotted Wolf of Heart Butte." *Great Falls Tribune*. A Gannett Company, n.d. Web. 29 Nov. 2014.

"Josephine Baker." *Bio.* A&E Television Networks, 2014. Web. 19 Nov. 2014.

"The Julia Child Foundation for Gastronomy and the Culinary Arts." *The Julia Child Foundation for Gastronomy and the Culinary Arts.* n.d. Web. 22 Oct. 2014.

Kantor, Jodi. "A Titan's How-To on Breaking the Glass Ceiling." *The New York Times.* The New York Times, 21 Feb. 2013. Web. 28 Nov. 2014.

King, Billie Jean, and Cynthia Starr. *We Have Come a Long Way: The Story of Women's Tennis.* New York: McGraw-Hill, 1988. Print.

Knizhnik, Shana. "Notorious R.B.G." *Notorious R.B.G.* Shana Knizhnik, n.d. Web. 10 Nov. 2014.

Krull, Kathleen, and Kathryn Hewitt. *Lives of Extraordinary Women: Rulers, Rebels (and What the Neighbors Thought).* San Diego: Harcourt, 2000. Print.

"Lea Salonga Biography." *PinoyStop.* PinoyStop, 08 Apr. 2006. Web. 28 Nov. 2014.

Lea Salonga Live. By Lea Salonga. The Philippine International Convention Center, Manila. 2000. Performance.

León, Vicki. *4,000 Years of Uppity Women: Rebellious Belles, Daring Dames, and Headstrong Heroines through the Ages.* New York: MJF, 2011. Print.

León, Vicki. *Outrageous Women of the Middle Ages.* New York: Wiley, 1998. Print.

Lewis, Jone J. "Josephine Baker Facts and Biography." *About Women's History.* N.d. Web. 19 Nov. 2014.

Louck, Tracie, and Barbara Haderman. "Biography." *The Official Josephine Baker Website.* CMG Worldwide, n.d. Web. 19 Nov. 2014.

"Madam C. J. Walker Official Website." *Madam C. J. Walker Official Website.* Madame C. J. Walker Enterprises, n.d. Web. 30 Nov. 2014.

Mankiller, Wilma. "Gifts of Speech." *Wilma Mankiller.* Gender Studies at Sweet Briar College, n.d. Web. 19 Nov. 2014.

Mankiller, Wilma Pearl, and Michael Wallis. *Mankiller: A*

Chief and Her People. New York: St. Martin's Griffin, 2000. Print.

"Marie Curie—Biographical." *Nobelprize.org.* The Nobel Prize, n.d. Web. 05 Nov. 2014.

"Mary Edmonia Lewis." *Bio.* A&E Television Networks, 2014. Web. 16 Nov. 2014.

McCann, Michelle Roehm, and Amelie Welden. *Girls Who Rocked the World: Heroines from Joan of Arc to Mother Teresa.* New York: Aladdin, 2012. Print.

McCarthy, Colman. *"What Would You Do If?" The Class of Nonviolence.* Washington, D.C.: Center for Teaching Peace, 2008. N. pag. Print.

McQueen, Keven. *Offbeat Kentuckians.* Kuttawa, KY: McClanahan Pub. House, 2001. Print.

Mikkelson, Barbara. "Julia Child Dropped the Turkey." *Urban Legends Reference Pages. Snopes.com,* n.d. Web. 23 Nov. 2014.

Minturn, Molly. "Girl Most Likely." *The University of Virginia Magazine.* University of Virginia, n.d. Web. 09 Nov. 2014.

Mishkin, Budd. *"One on 1 Profile: CEO of Girl Scouts USA Anna Maria Chavez Leads the 100-Plus-Year-Old Organization into the 21st Century."* Time Warner Cable News 1 New York, 31 Mar. 2014. Web. 22 Oct. 2014.

Moore, Deborah Dash, and Paula E. Hyman. *Jewish Women in America: A Historical Encyclopedia.* New York: Routledge, 1998. Print.

Morais, Betsy. "Ada Lovelace, the First Tech Visionary—The New Yorker." *The New Yorker.* Condé Nast, 15 Oct. 2013. Web. 15 Nov. 2014.

Newberg, Julie. "ASU Advisor Diane Humetewa Named 1st American Indian Woman Federal Judge." *ASU News.* Arizona State University, 15 May 2014. Web. 11 Nov. 2014.

"1993—Mary & Carrie Dann." *Right Livelihood Award.* The Right Livelihood Award Foundation, n.d. Web. 09 Nov. 2014.

"The Official Site of Hedy Lamarr." *The Official Site of Hedy Lamarr.* CMG Worldwide, n.d. Web. 14 Nov. 2014.

Orman, Suze. "About Suze." *Orman: The Personal & Professional*

Biography of a Financial Powerhouse. Suze Orman, n.d. Web. 21 Nov. 2014.

Ouimette-Kinney, Mary. "Mary G. Ross." *Biographies of Women Mathematicians.* Agnes Scott College, n.d. Web. 11 Nov. 2014.

Parker, Dorothy, and Stuart Y. Silverstein. *Not Much Fun: The Lost Poems of Dorothy Parker.* New York: Scribner, 2009. Print.

Pascale, Jordan. "Susan La Flesche's Legacy Lives On." *Native Daughters.* University of Nebraska-Lincoln, n.d. Web. 22 Nov. 2014.

Pelisek, Christine. "Etta James's Son Donto Says Addiction Was Part of Famed Singer's Life." *The Daily Beast.* Newsweek/Daily Beast, 15 Nov. 2012. Web. 12 Nov. 2014.

Petersen, Anne Helen. *Scandals of Classic Hollywood.* New York: Penguin Group USA, 2014. Print.

Pettinger, Tejvan. "Biography: Tegla Loroupe." *Biography Online.* Tejvan Pettinger, n.d. Web. 15 Nov. 2014.

"Photograph of Private Minnie Spotted Wolf." *Blackfoot Digital Library.* Red Crow Community College, n.d. Web. 29 Nov. 2014.

Porath, Jason. "Ranavalona I." *Rejected Princesses.* Jason Porath, n.d. Web. 01 Dec. 2014.

Quinn, Susan. *Marie Curie: A Life.* Reading, MA: Addison-Wesley, 1996. Print.

Rai, Aishwarya (@AishwaryaRai) "Every girl needs to recognise that she herself is a beacon of hope and has the potential to influence her future." 08 Feb. 2013. 9:13 AM. Tweet.

Reese, Lyn. "Empress Wu Zetian." *Women in World History Curriculum.* U.S. Department of Education, n.d. Web. 01 Dec. 2014.

Rhodes, Richard. *Hedy's Folly: The Life and Breakthrough Inventions of Hedy Lamarr, the Most Beautiful Woman in the World.* New York: Vintage, 2012. Print.

Rich, Doris L. *Queen Bess: Daredevil Aviator.* Washington: Smithsonian Institution, 1993. Print.

Rolka, Gail Meyer. *100 Women Who Shaped World History.* San

Francisco: Bluewood, 1994. Print.

Rose, Lacey. "The Booming Business of Ellen DeGeneres."
The Hollywood Reporter. Prometheus Global Media, 22 Aug.
2012. Print.

"Ruth Bader Ginsburg." *The Oyez Project.* IIT Chicago-Kent
College of Law, n.d. Web. 09 Nov. 2014.

Said, Carolyn. "Q&A with Personal Financial Guru Suze Orman." *SFGate.* Hearst Communications, n.d. Web. 23 Nov.
2014.

Sandberg, Sheryl. *Lean In: Women, Work, and the Will to Lead.*
New York: Alfred A Knopf, 2013. Print.

Sandberg, Sheryl, and Jimmy Rollins. "Sheryl Sandberg /
Jimmy Rollins | Ep. 1 | Win/Win." *AOL Win/Win.* AOL
Originals, 7 Nov. 2014. Web. 28 Nov. 2014.

Sandberg, Sheryl. "Why We Have Too Few Women Leaders."
TED. Sapling Foundation, 10 Dec. 2010. Web. 28 Nov.
2014.

Schaller, Kb. *100 Native American Women Who Changed the
World.* S.l.: Peppertree, 2013. Print.

Scheader, Catherine. *Shirley Chisholm: Teacher and Congress-
woman.* Hillsdale, NJ: Enslow, 1990. Print.

Schwartz, Larry. "Billie Jean Won for All Women." *ESPN.*
ESPN Internet Ventures, n.d. Web. 11 Nov. 2014.

Secrets of Egypt's Lost Queen. Dir. Brando Quilici. Discovery—
Gaiam, 2007. DVD.

Severo, Richard. "Estée Lauder, Pursuer of Beauty And Cosmetics Titan, Dies at 97." *The New York Times.* The New
York Times, 25 Apr. 2004. Web. 14 Nov. 2014.

"Shirley Chisholm." *ABC News.* ABC News Network, 02 Feb.
2006. Web. 23 Nov. 2014.

Skard, Torild. *Women of Power: Half a Century of Female Presi-
dents and Prime Ministers Worldwide.* Bristol: Policy, 2014.
Print.

Stanton, Andrew, Lee Unkrich, Graham Walters, John Las-
seter, Bob Peterson, David Reynolds, Albert Brooks,
Ellen DeGeneres, Alexander Gould, Willem Dafoe, Brad

Garrett, Allison Janney, Austin Pendleton, Stephen Root, Vicki Lewis, Joe Ranft, Geoffrey Rush, Elizabeth Perkins, Nicholas Bird, Barry Humphries, Eric Bana, Bruce Spence, Bill Hunter, LuLu Ebeling, Jordy Ranft, Erica Beck, Erik P. Sullivan, John Ratzenberger, Thomas Newman, David I. Salter, Ralph Eggleston, Sharon Calahan, Jeremy Lasky, and Thomas Pasatieri. *Finding Nemo*. Burbank, Calif: Buena Vista Home Entertainment, 2003. Film.

Stern, Ray. "Diane Humetewa, Hopi Indian From Arizona, Makes History as New Federal Judge." *Valley Fever*. Phoenix New Times, 15 May 2014. Web. 11 Nov. 2014.

Strzemien, Anya. "Michigan Girl Scout Sells 17,328 Boxes of Cookies." *The Huffington Post. TheHuffingtonPost.com*, 15 May 2008. Web. 05 Oct. 2014.

Tallchief, Maria, and Larry Kaplan. *Maria Tallchief: America's Prima Ballerina*. New York: Henry Holt, 1997. Print.

Tegla Loroupe Peace Foundation. Tegla Loroupe Peace Foundation, n.d. Web. 15 Nov. 2014.

Thimmesh, Catherine, and Melissa Sweet. *Girls Think of Everything: Stories of Ingenious Inventions by Women*. Boston: Houghton Mifflin, 2000. Print.

"3 Black Women Who Helped Shape the Old West." *Female Talk*. Neon Gecko, 22 Feb. 2011. Web. 30 Nov. 2014.

Todd, Anne M. *Vera Wang*. New York: Chelsea House, 2007. Print.

Tyler, Royall. "Murasaki Shikibu." *Harvard Magazine*. Harvard University, June 2002. Print.

United States. National Park Service. "Picotte Memorial Hospital, Featured in National American Indian Heritage Month." *National Parks Service*. U.S. Department of the Interior, n.d. Web. 23 Nov. 2014.

Walker, Alice. "Alice Walker's Garden." *Alice Walker: The Official Website*. Alice Walker, n.d. Web. 30 Nov. 2014.

"Walker Theatre." *Walker Theatre*. Madame Walker Theatre Center, n.d. Web. 30 Nov. 2014.

Wells, Ida B. *Southern Horrors: Lynch Law in All Its Phases*.

New York: New York Age, 1892. Print.

White, Cody. "Minnie Spotted Wolf and the Marine Corps." *The National Archives.* United States National Archives, n.d. Web. 29 Nov. 2014.

White, Evelyn C. *Alice Walker: A Life.* New York: Norton, 2006. Print.

Willard, Charity C., ed., *The "Livre de Paix" of Christine de Pisan: A Critical Edition.* The Hague: Mouton, 1958.

"Wu Zetian." *ChinaCulture.org.* Ministry of Culture, China, n.d. Web. 01 Dec. 2014.

Yoo, Paula, and Lin Wang. *Shining Star: The Anna May Wong Story.* New York: Lee & Low, 2009. Print.

Recommended Reading

Abdul-Jabbar, Kareem, Raymond Obstfeld, Ben Boos, and AG Ford. *What Color Is My World?: The Lost History of African-American Inventors.* Somerville, MA: Candlewick, 2012. Print.

Beaton, Kate. *Hark!: A Vagrant.* Montréal: Drawn & Quarterly, 2011. Print.

Chin-Lee, Cynthia, Megan Halsey, and Sean Addy. *Amelia to Zora: Twenty-Six Women Who Changed the World.* Watertown, MA: Charlesbridge, 2005. Print.

Harness, Cheryl. *Remember the Ladies: 100 Great American Women.* New York: HarperCollins, 2001. Print.

Heinemann, Sue. *The New York Public Library Amazing Women in American History: A Book of Answers for Kids.* New York: Wiley, 1998. Print.

León, Vicki. *Outrageous Women of the Middle Ages.* New York: Wiley, 1998. Print.

McCann, Michelle Roehm, and Amelie Welden. *Girls Who Rocked the World: Heroines from Joan of Arc to Mother Teresa.* New York: Aladdin, 2012. Print.

Ragan, Kathleen, and Jane Yolen. *Fearless Girls, Wise Women, and Beloved Sisters: Heroines in Folktales from around the World.* New York: W. W. Norton, 2000. Print.

Thimmesh, Catherine, and Melissa Sweet. *Girls Think of Everything: Stories of Ingenious Inventions by Women.* Boston: Houghton Mifflin, 2000. Print.

Yolen, Jane, and Susan Guevara. *Not One Damsel in Distress: World Folktales for Strong Girls.* San Diego: Silver Whistle, 2000. Print.

Acknowledgments

There are far too many people who went into making this book a reality, and for everyone I manage to forget, please forgive me! Many thanks to my mother Sheryl Jern, who taught me to love to read, to Mom Bettis, who introduced me to the wider world of feminism when I was a tween, and to my daughters Nikki and Gwen, my aunts Melody and Jinni, and my grandmothers Aldith and Joan, for making me the woman I am today.

I'm so very grateful for my agent, Jim McCarthy, who never blinks when I drop a random proposal in his mail. He's an extraordinary cheerleader and the best advocate a writer could want. Huge thanks to my editor, Dana Bergman, who brought amazing ideas and enthusiasm to this project—I asked for only one book, but she gave me two. When does that ever happen?

Finally, endless thanks to the entire team at Puffin for creating beautiful books, and to Cara Petrus for expertly illustrating it all. I'm pretty sure the reference pictures of statues were exactly not helpful at all, but hopefully, it was fun figuring out how to use them!   —SM

I am ever grateful to my husband, Steve, who is the best studio assistant/life partner a gal could hope for. Thanks for always making dinner and scanning sketches and line art.

My agent, Nancy Moore, is nothing but the steadfast best. The lady works hard, has my back, and believes in me. Eileen Kreit, Dana Bergman, Irene Vandervoort, and the entire Puffin team, you are wonderful to collaborate with and I blush at your compliments—thank you.

Finally, Saundra Mitchell, thanks for writing smart books for smart kids. Also, you gave me the opportunity to draw portrait after portrait, and few things are better in a day in this illustrator's life— thank you.   —CP